The Book of Daniel

Explorations in Christian Scripture

Cypress Bible Study Series

Ed Gallagher

Illustrated by
Josiah Gallagher

HERITAGE
CHRISTIAN UNIVERSITY
PRESS

Catalog in Publication

Gallagher, Ed (Edmon Louis), 1979-
The book of Daniel: explorations in Christian scripture/ Ed Gallagher Cypress
Study series
p. cm.
Includes scripture index.
1. Bible. Daniel—Criticism, interpretation, etc. I. Author. II. Title. III. Series.
224.506 DDC21
ISBN: 978-1-956811-80-3 (pbk.) ; 978-1-956811-81-0 (ebook).

Library of Congress Control Number: 2024948945

Artwork by Josiah Gallagher.

Cover designed by Brad McKinnon and Brittany Vander Maas.

For more information:

Heritage Christian University
PO Box HCU
3625 Helton Drive
Florence, AL 35630

www.hcu.edu/publications

In memory of
Ronny Stubblefield,
a good and faithful servant

Contents

Preface

For the spring quarter of the year 2020, I decided that the adult classes at the Sherrod Ave. Church of Christ in Florence, Alabama would study the book of Daniel. That lasted all of two weeks. Already at the beginning of the quarter, which started in March, I had begun hearing about a new disease that was beginning to worry some people. By the third week of the spring quarter, I was in a makeshift TV studio in the church's library, where the incomparable Ginger Leigh was recording me teaching through the text of Daniel for a video series that would be released week-by-week on Sundays for our congregation. That was the unforgettable—and hopefully unrepeated—origin of this book.

Daniel is a difficult book, deceptively difficult. The first six chapters are so familiar to most Christians, even very young ones, that we might think that the book is filled with children's stories. While the stories in the first half of the book present complexities of their own, it's the second half of the book where the real difficulties lie. Some Christians spend all their time here, in apocalyptic visions of Daniel 7–12, trying to relate these ancient prophecies to today's headlines, attempting to discern how close to the end times we live. Other Christians avoid these visions like the plague. This book encourages a different approach. I do not think that God gave us the apocalyptic visions in order to map out a scheme of the end of history, but he most definitely intended for believers to read and value these chapters. While I acknowledge that the reading strategy I propose in this book is not void of its own share of complexity, I have tried not only to explain the nature of the visions and some of their details but also to show how they can help us cope with life as it is now.

Several people have offered valuable assistance with this book. My oldest daughter, Miriam, read through the entire book and provided comments. So did my friend, John Young. My boss, Nathan Daily, also offered comments on some parts of the book. Brad McKinnon, Brittany VanderMaas, and Jamie Cox have performed their usual admirable work in producing this book, and I am as ever grateful for their dedication and diligence. Terry Stubblefield early on expressed interest in this material, and has now had to wait four years for its completion despite my repeated assurances that I'd be done with it soon. (I have learned to use "soon" in the same way as Jesus.)

The book is dedicated to his brother, Ronny Stubblefield, who put up with a lot of nonsense from me and some others (yes, you, Ryan) when he served as our youth minister in the 1990s at the Pennyrile Church of Christ in Madisonville, Kentucky. Ronny was one of the great influences on my life, who was never a full-time minister but always dedicated a great amount of time and energy to the church. He was a model Christian servant, a great teacher, and a dedicated husband to Cindy and a caring father to David and Jon. I am proud that he found some of my books useful in his teaching ministry at Pennyrile. I wish he could have used this one. I miss him.

My wife, Jodi, and our children—Miriam, Evelyn, Josiah, Jasmine, Marvin, and Ellie—have provided the supportive and joyful environment that allows projects like this to seem valuable and worthwhile. To my son, Josiah Gallagher, I extend deep gratitude for his drawing the pictures included here before each chapter, and for drawing the book's cover art. By the time this book is published, he'll be 16 years old. I appreciate his artistic talent, his diligence, and his willingness to incorporate some of my ideas. Thank you, son.

Introduction

The book of Daniel gives instructions on how to live faithfully in a pagan world. Thus, it is a book for our time. The book encourages realism: your faith will conflict with the world around you, and the pagan empire will try to compel you to conform—or it will kill you. The book encourages perseverance: when the pagan empire tries to kill you, be faithful unto death. And the book encourages hope: one day God will turn everything upside down. These three key elements of the book of Daniel (realism, perseverance, hope) provide an apt summary for all of Scripture.

The book of Daniel can be divided in a couple of different ways: by content or by language. (See the table on the next page.) Taking the issue of language first, the book of Daniel is one of the few books in the Hebrew Bible that contains Aramaic alongside its Hebrew. Both of these languages are written in the same alphabet, so you can't really tell that the language changes unless you know the language (that is, they look just alike on the page). Hebrew and Aramaic are related languages, but they're also distinct, like English and French. Being able to read one does not mean that you can read the other (cf. 2 Kgs 18:26), though there are a lot of similarities. Aramaic appears in the Hebrew Bible in Ezra (4:8–6:18; 7:12–26), in Jeremiah (10:11), and a little bit in

Genesis (31:47), but more in Daniel than anywhere else. The Aramaic portion starts in the middle of a verse: when the Chaldeans respond to Nebuchadnezzar in 2:4, the text says they respond in Aramaic. All of the book up to that point (1:1–2:4a) is in Hebrew, but the response of the Chaldeans is in Aramaic, and the stories stay in Aramaic until the end of chapter 7.

Content:

Chapters 1–6	Chapters 7–12
Children's Bible Stories	Apocalyptic Visions

Language:

Chapter 1	Chapters 2–7	Chapters 8–12
Hebrew	Aramaic	Hebrew

It's not at all clear why half of Daniel is written in Aramaic. Some scholars have guessed that maybe the whole book was originally written in Aramaic and the beginning and end were translated into Hebrew; others have thought that the book was originally written in two languages for some reason.[1] But those are just guesses; all we have are guesses. Why would an author want to switch languages like that? It would be like writing an introduction and conclusion in English and then putting a big block of French right in the middle.

Sometimes we see something like that, don't we?—English-language movies with some bits in a foreign language, say, a spy speaking Russian or German to his bosses, and the movie doesn't supply a translation. What's that supposed to communicate? Actually, maybe we should reverse the roles, since Aramaic at the time, like English today, was the international language, whereas Hebrew was the language of one particular people. Aramaic had

---

1. See the summary of views in John J. Collins, *Daniel*, Hermeneia (Minneapolis: Fortress, 1993), 12–13.

been adopted by the Assyrians as a language of administration around 700 BC, and Aramaic retained this position (alongside Akkadian) for the Babylonians and also for the Persians. So maybe the language issue in Daniel is a bit like *The Two Popes*. Have you seen that movie on Netflix, about, you know, two popes? It starts with people speaking Latin, and Spanish, and Italian, and German, whatever would be the natural language for that particular person, and then at some point, it switches to English, after already establishing that they weren't really speaking English but some other language. Maybe, in Daniel, there's a point to the changing of the languages. Maybe the book uses the language of empire (Aramaic) while discussing the empire, and then it uses Hebrew on the bookends to establish the reader's position within a different empire, not the empires of the world, which will all come tumbling down.[2] In that sense, the language switching corresponds to themes within the book.

The other easy way of dividing the book—the one more obvious to English speakers—is based on the genre of the text. It begins with tales of our heroes and ends with strange visions. The first six chapters are well-known, the last six ... not so much. Both the stories and the visions have the same basic theme: be faithful to God, be patient, God will set all things right.

The stories in the first six chapters are of basically two kinds: stories of bravery and stories of interpretation. There are three chapters that involve offering an interpretation of some mystery (chs. 2, 4, 5), and each time the wise men of Babylon prove to be completely useless and Daniel must come and interpret the mystery. The other three chapters in this section display the importance of bravery, whether that involves young teenagers standing up to a king by refusing to eat his fancy food (ch. 1), or refusing to bow down to an idol (ch. 3), or an old man refusing to

---

2. For a position similar to this one, see Anathea E. Portier-Young, "Languages of Identity and Obligation: Daniel as Bilingual Book," *Vetus Testamentum* 60 (2010): 98–115.

pray to the human king (ch. 6). In each case, the bravery—the
faithfulness—of the heroes is rewarded by God.

The strange visions in the second half of the book are
written in a genre called apocalyptic. It's the same style of
writing as in the book of Revelation, and it's the book of Revelation that gives the genre its name. The Greek word for "revelation" is "apocalypse" (ἀποκάλυψις, *apokalypsis*). So what we say
about how to read the visions of Daniel is largely relevant also
for reading Revelation, and studying the book of Daniel is the
best preparation for studying Revelation. In fact, the book of
Revelation—without ever quoting the Old Testament—
constantly borrows imagery from Daniel (and Ezekiel and other
books).

These visions in Daniel (and Revelation) are supposed to be
"revelations" or "unveilings." They are supposed to reveal (not
conceal!) the way things really are. They pull back the curtain on
our world and show us what is really going on. They reveal how
God views things, and they reveal the heavenly struggle mirrored
in earthly conflicts.

Apocalyptic writing is distinct from classical prophecy in a
few ways:

- the medium of divine communication. In classical
  prophecy, often "the word of the Lord" came directly
  to the prophet somehow. In apocalyptic, there's
  usually an angel that brings information.
- the subject matter. Apocalyptic literature often deals
  with the end of the age (not the end of time!),
  whereas classical prophecy often deals with
  contemporary times or the near future (e.g., the
  threat of coming punishment).
- imagery. Apocalyptic literature often reports strange
  visions. This is not characteristic of classical
  prophecy.

- theme. The classical prophets usually called on people to repent of their sins and secondarily held out hope for the faithful. In apocalyptic literature, hope is front and center. Daniel encourages perseverance and faithfulness. There is much less emphasis on repentance here (but see ch. 9), because Daniel and his three friends have little need for repentance.

Mark Hamilton proposes a structure for the book of Daniel whereby the Aramaic section has a chiastic arrangement.[3]

ch. 1: Introduction

chs. 2–7: Daniel vs. Foreign Rulers—chiastic, almost completely Aramaic

a. Nebuchadnezzar's Dream: Four Empires Destroyed by God's Kingdom (ch. 2)

b. Fiery Furnace: The Faith of Daniel's Friends Tested (ch. 3)

c. Nebuchadnezzar's humiliation (ch. 4)

c´. Belshazzar's humiliation (ch. 5)

b´. Lion's Den: The Faith of Daniel Tested (ch. 6)

a´. Daniel's Vision: Four Empires Destroyed by God's Kingdom (ch. 7)

chs. 8–12: World crises and final renewal

There are difficult historical issues in the book of Daniel. The book talks about four empires, without naming them, and the identity of those empires has exercised interpreters since the book was written. The very beginning of the book mentions a time of captivity during the reign of King Jehoiakim of Judah, a captivity otherwise unattested. The character named Darius the Mede, who ruled during the "Lion's Den" chapter (ch. 6), is unknown outside the book of Daniel. These various historical

---

3. Mark W. Hamilton, *A Theological Introduction to the Old Testament* (Oxford: Oxford University Press, 2018), 332.

problems that have led to much scholarly work and speculation will not occupy us in this book.[4] In spite of these difficulties and the debates they inspire, the main theme in the book of Daniel —encouraging people to live righteously in the face of persecution—comes through clearly.

The book of Daniel was very popular in ancient Judaism and Christianity. Its language had a decisive impact on the way Jesus described himself (Son of Man!) and the trial that led to his Crucifixion (see Mark 14:62; cf. Dan 7:13–14). While many Old Testament books are important for a proper understanding of the Christian religion, few are more important than the book of Daniel.

---

4. For a conservative treatment of these issues, see Alan R. Millard, "Daniel in Babylon: An Accurate Record?" in *Do Historical Matters Matter to Faith? A Critical Appraisal of Modern and Postmodern Approaches to Scripture*, ed. James K. Hoffmeier and Dennis R. Magary (Wheaton, IL: Crossway, 2012), 263–80.

Chapter 1
Vegetables and Water

Do not be conformed to this world, but be transformed by the renewing of your minds, so that you may discern what is the will of God—what is good and acceptable and perfect (Rom 12:2).

Today the message that blares out at us from our culture is, "Be yourself!" "You do you." "You're perfect the way you are." I think this is a new thing. When I was growing up, and I guess from all of human history before that point, the message was some version of, "You need to conform." And now the message is, "Don't conform." Well, I should say the overt, stated message is, "Don't conform," but, you know, the more things change, the more they stay the same. I would say the requirement for conformity is perhaps now even greater with this new style of messaging, "don't conform." That is, the message "don't conform" seems to mean "don't conform to the attitudes you may have been taught, but do conform to what Hollywood thinks." Now with cancel culture, etc., it seems like the requirement for conformity is more intense than it's ever been.

The Book of Daniel is a book about conformity, and the resistance to it. I guess we could say that Daniel and his friends embody the 21st-century messaging, "Be yourself" and "You do you" better than most anyone in the 21st century. From the very beginning of the book, when they are introduced to us as young men, probably teenagers, they resist the call to conform to the brave new world of the Babylonian court, which exercises its power with both a carrot (food and wine) and a stick (fiery furnace, anyone?). Despite the cancel culture all around them, they commit themselves to living according to the ways of their God and letting the chips fall where they may.

Historical Setup

> Serve the king of Babylon and live (Jer 27:17).

The Book of Daniel begins with a reference to the Babylonian King Nebuchadnezzar and the Judean King Jehoiakim. The situation is the one we read about in 2 Kings 24–25. The Assyrian Empire has recently suffered the fatal blows inflicted by the Babylonians, so that the position of dominant empire has shifted now from Assyria to Babylon. A convenient date to remember in this regard is 612 BC, the date of the destruction of the city of Nineveh, the capital of Assyria. It had been Assyria, a century or more earlier, that had taken the northern nation of Israel (the ten tribes) into captivity (2 Kgs 17) in 722 BC. Judah survived until the rise of the next empire, Babylon. At the time of Nineveh's destruction, the king in Judah was Josiah (2 Kgs 22–23). He had three sons and a grandson come to the throne.

- Jehoahaz, son of Josiah (2 Kgs 23:30–35). He reigned only three months following the death of his father. The king of Egypt held him captive and installed his brother Eliakim (= Jehoiakim) on the throne.
- Jehoiakim, son of Josiah (2 Kgs 23:36–24:7). His name had been Eliakim (23:34), but the king of Egypt changed it. He reigned for eleven years. He seems to

have died of natural causes (24:6) right at the time that the Babylonians were getting fed up with him and making plans to attack.

- Jehoiachin, son of Jehoiakim (2 Kgs 24:8–17). He reigned for only three months (like his uncle Jehoahaz). Nebuchadnezzar attacked Jerusalem and carried off many of the temple treasures (24:13) and a whole bunch of people, including Jehoiachin, the king. In his place, Nebuchadnezzar installed Jehoiachin's uncle, Mattaniah (= Zedekiah), on the throne. Jehoiachin lived in exile for decades and was eventually given a privileged position at the king's table in Babylon (25:27–30).

- Zedekiah, son of Josiah (2 Kgs 24:18–25:7). He was the last king of Judah and the third and final son of Josiah to reign. His name had been Mattaniah (24:17) but Nebuchadnezzar changed it. He reigned for eleven years (like his brother Jehoiakim). He witnessed the Babylonian takeover of Jerusalem, the destruction of the temple and walls, and the murder of his sons before his own eyes were removed (25:6). He was taken captive to Babylon (25:7), where (presumably) he died.

The capture of Jehoiachin and the first wave of captivity of the people of Jerusalem occurred in 597 BC. The destruction of the temple and the city occurred in 586 BC. This is the Babylonian exile. The book of Jeremiah also mentions a third wave of exile in 582 BC (Jer 52:28–30).

The Book of Daniel mentions a small-scale wave of exile (otherwise unknown) in the third year of Jehoiakim, which would have been around 606 BC, right around the time that Nebuchadnezzar became king, replacing his father Nabopolassar (but most often Nebuchadnezzar's ascension is dated to 605 or

604).[1]

It is important to note what the text says at Daniel 1:2—
"YHWH let King Jehoiakim of Judah fall into his [= Nebuchadnezzar's] power." Lest we think that Nebuchadnezzar is in
control, the text immediately assures us that he is not. Rather, it
is the God in whom the Judeans had failed to trust who main-
tains control, even directing Nebuchadnezzar's take-over of
Jerusalem. Jeremiah the prophet had actually called Nebuchadnezzar the servant of YHWH on multiple occasions (cf. Jer 25:9;
27:6; 43:10).

By the way, the land of Shinar (1:2) is another name for
Babylon (Gen 10:10; 11:2; Zech 5:11).

Daniel and Food

> Do not desire the ruler's delicacies,
>   for they are deceptive food (Prov 23:3).

In this early wave of exile, Daniel was taken along with his
friends Hananiah, Mishael, and Azariah (Dan 1:6). They had
been a part of the upper classes in Jerusalem (1:3).[2] Already at

---

1. For a treatment of this historical difficulty, see Alan R. Millard, "Daniel in
Babylon: An Accurate Record?" in *Do Historical Matters Matter to Faith? A Critical
Appraisal of Modern and Postmodern Approaches to Scripture*, ed. James K. Hoffmeier
and Dennis R. Magary (Wheaton, IL: Crossway, 2012), 263–80, at 263–66. Josephus, *Antiquities of the Jews* 10.186–88, associates Daniel with the reign of
Zedekiah, apparently in response to the historical difficulty created by the book;
see Jay Braverman, *Jerome's Commentary on Daniel: A Study of Comparative Jewish
and Christian Interpretations of the Hebrew Bible* (Washington, D.C.: The Catholic
Biblical Association of America, 1978), 64 n. 54.

2. In Dan 1:3, the title of Ashpenaz could be translated as "chief eunuch," as it is
in the Septuagint. There is a prominent tradition in ancient Judaism and Christianity that Daniel and his three friends were made eunuchs at this time, in
fulfillment of Isaiah 39:7. For references to this tradition, see Braverman, *Jerome's
Commentary on Daniel*, 53–66. Josephus, *Antiquities of the Jews* 10.186, states that
some of the captives were made eunuchs, but does not say it specifically in reference to Daniel and his friends. For ancient traditions on the ancestry of Daniel
and his friends, see Braverman, *Jerome's Commentary on Daniel*, 66–71.

this time, they are described as "versed in every branch of wisdom, endowed with knowledge and insight, and competent to serve in the king's palace," in addition to being physically attractive (1:4). They were being trained for leadership in Jerusalem. They'll get their chance in Babylon.[3]

This group of friends refuses to eat the royal food (1:8). Why? According to Carol Newsom, "Why Daniel should consider the king's food defiling has never been definitively explained."[4] We can imagine some reasons. Perhaps the meat would not have been prepared in the proper way, with its blood drained, as prescribed in Leviticus (17:10–16). The word "defiling" points in this direction; it seems to indicate that it's not just that Daniel and his friends didn't want the food, but that it would render them unclean. The Bible sometimes presents unclean food as a fact of life in exile (Hos 9:3). But that reason wouldn't really explain why Daniel prefers water to wine. The Bible describes no kosher method for producing wine.[5] There are today kosher ways of producing wine, and these rules go back to the rabbinic period, but almost certainly not to the period of Daniel.[6] According to Yonatan Adler,

> The fact that not only the royal food but also the king's *wine* was regarded as problematic mitigates against the possibility

---

3. For a study of Judean exiles in Babylon, see the open-access book Tero Alstola, *Judeans in Babylon: A Study of Deportees in Sixth and Fifth Centuries BCE* (Leiden: Brill, 2020). The second chapter is called "Judean Royalty and Professionals in Babylon."

4. Carol A. Newsom and Brennan W. Breed, *Daniel*, Old Testament Library (Louisville: WJK, 2014), 47.

5. It could be that Daniel opposed drinking "Gentile wine" because "in ancient cultures people poured libations to their gods whenever they drank wine," according to the suggestion of E. P. Sanders, *Jewish Law from Jesus to the Mishnah: Five Studies* (Philadelphia: TPI, 1990), 273; see also p. 24.

6. Wikipedia: "Kashrut." Search on the webpage for "wine." The rabbinic prohibition against drinking Gentile wine is found in the Mishnah (*m. Avodah Zarah* 2.3). The Talmud (commenting on the relevant mishnah) derives justification for the prohibition from Deuteronomy 32:38 (*b. Avodah Zarah* 29b, at §10 of the online Talmud at sefaria.org).

that Pentateuchal dietary prohibitions might be at stake, as
these include no sweeping proscriptions against wine or other
beverages (although these might be liable to ritual impurity).[7]

So maybe Daniel's refusal to eat the royal meat and royal
wine wasn't so much about adhering to a particular commandment in the Torah but rather had other motivations. After all,
the Bible presents the opportunity for the exiled king
Jechoiachin to eat at the king's table to be a great honor (2 Kgs
25:29–30). The Bible doesn't exactly say what Esther ate or drank
while she was being (ahem!) interviewed by the Persian king and,
later, once she was queen, but Scripture certainly doesn't represent her as taking a stand on these matters.[8] Nor Nehemiah the
cupbearer. Perhaps it would have been technically okay for
Daniel and his friends to eat along with the other trainees.

So why resist the rich food and wine? Clearly this is not a
case that aligns with Paul's statement, "Some believe in eating
anything, while the weak eat only vegetables" (Rom 14:2), but
just the opposite; in the case of Daniel and his friends, it is those
who are strong in spirit who are eating only vegetables. I've seen
the suggestion that Daniel might want to identify with his exiled
fellow Jews who were not offered cushy positions in the Babylonian king's court, so he chose to eat the food of slaves instead
of the food of kings. Another suggestion is that he's mourning
over the destruction of Jerusalem, and so he declines the food of
celebration (cf. Dan 6:18; 10:2–3). I like these suggestions, but I
like another suggestion better (a suggestion that does not stand
opposed to these other proposals but could work with them).

I think Daniel's refusal to eat the king's food was a way of
resisting conformity to the ways of Babylon. Perhaps Daniel did

---

7. Yonatan Adler, *The Origins of Judaism: An Archaeological-Historical Reappraisal*
(New Haven, CT: Yale University Press, 2022), 42.
8. On the other hand, in the apocrypha, Tobit won't eat the food of the
Gentiles (Tob 1:10–13) and Judith refuses to eat or drink what is provided by
Gentiles (Judith 12:1–2).

not want to express complete loyalty to the king the way everyone else was doing. We know that benefits, gifts, often come with strings attached. When Don Corleone gives you a gift, he's going to expect loyalty in return. Maybe that's what Daniel doesn't want to get involved in. There is no doubt that Nebuchadnezzar's plan is to turn these Judean young men into full-fledged Babylonians. So he teaches them the literature and the language of the Chaldeans (1:4), gives them a nice place to stay and great food (1:5). He's getting them used to the lifestyle. He's using the carrot to hasten conformity.

Daniel doesn't want to conform.

So he picks his battle. Food. That's the part of his life that he's going to control. Or, rather, that's the part of his life that will be a sign to him and everyone else that he's not just like all the other Judean youths soaking up their newfound privilege with the pagan king. Daniel's aims are different; his life is dedicated to a different cause, to a different service. He won't be a court prophet or court wise man. He's going to be his own man, God's man, not Nebuchadnezzar's man.

It seems to me that this way of looking at Daniel 1 coheres with what we read in Leviticus.

> I am YHWH your God; I have separated you from the peoples. You shall therefore make a distinction between the clean animal and the unclean, and between the unclean bird and the clean; you shall not bring abomination on yourselves by animal or by bird or by anything with which the ground teems, which I have set apart for you to hold unclean. You shall be holy to me; for I YHWH am holy, and I have separated you from the other peoples to be mine (Lev 20:24–26).

Doesn't this passage seem to declare that one of the purposes of the Levitical food laws was to separate the Israelites from other people? Whether or not Daniel encountered forbidden foods in the king's court, he still needed to enact this purpose of

the food laws. He needed to resist conformity to the ways of
Babylon.

Conformity

Daniel wouldn't conform to the dominant culture. Do we? How
can we resist conforming to the dominant culture? How does the
dominant culture want us to conform? Which parts should we
resist? I can think of a few areas where we might want to think
about our lives.

1. Food. Daniel chose to resist the royal food. On a daily
   basis we probably eat about as well as
   Nebuchadnezzar. And our culture is paying for it in
   many ways. Maybe, like Daniel, we should turn over
   our eating habits to God. (I am not in any way
   promoting the Daniel Fast for health benefits.) On
   the one hand, the constant presence of food in our
   lives engenders food lust in us, constant attention to
   the desires of the flesh. On the other hand, our food
   industry is increasingly exploitative of both workers
   and land.[9] Think Wendell Berry.
2. Consumerism. The dominant culture tells us to spend
   all the money we make on junk and we'll be happy.
   Jesus tells us to do other things with our money (Matt
   6:1–4; Luke 16:19–31).
3. Appearances. Jesus had some pretty negative things to
   say about the way his contemporaries projected an
   image of themselves (Matt 6:1–18). How do his words
   relate to our use of social media?

---

9. This second idea is hinted at in connection to Daniel in Mark W. Hamilton,
A Theological Introduction to the Old Testament (Oxford: Oxford University Press,
2018), 333. For much more, see Norman Wirzba, *Food and Faith: A Theology of
Eating*, 2d ed. (Cambridge: Cambridge University Press, 2019).

I think it is fair to say that in each of these ways—and many, many more—the dominant culture in our day demands conformity. Daniel provides an example of someone resisting such conformity, even if in a small way. But Daniel wasn't alone; he had his little community of friends. The church is supposed to be an alternative community, resisting the pressures of society and encouraging its members to do the same.

When the culture demands conformity, Daniel ate only vegetables and water. The church also needs to find ways to encourage one another to resist the demands of the dominant culture and submit to God.

Discussion Questions

- Who is King Jehoiakim? What do we know about his reign? See 2 Kings 23:36–24:7.
- Describe Daniel's family background.
- Why do the Babylonians give the Jewish boys new names?
- Why does Daniel not want to eat the king's food?
- What effect does Daniel's diet have on him and his friends? Why does it have this effect? Is it a natural effect or is it supernatural?

Chapter 2
The Coming Kingdom

Have you not known? Have you not heard?
 Has it not been told you from the beginning?
 Have you not understood from the foundations of the earth?
 It is he who sits above the circle of the earth,
 and its inhabitants are like grasshoppers;
 who stretches out the heavens like a curtain,
 and spreads them like a tent to live in;
 who brings princes to naught,
 and makes rulers of the earth as nothing.
 Scarcely are they planted, scarcely sown,
 scarcely has their stem taken root in the earth,
 when he blows upon them, and they wither,
 and the tempest carries them off like stubble
 (Isa 40:21–24).

At the time you're reading this, are people in America gearing up for the next big election? Of course, they are! Maybe you are too. To the extent that cable news and online news have become major sources of entertainment for Americans, not to mention talk radio, we are constantly reminded of the importance of politics. Each thing the president does or says, each thing Congress fails to do, each case decided by the Supreme Court, has earth-shattering, life-altering, history-making consequences.

The Book of Daniel wants to re-orient the way we think about politics. (So does the book of Revelation, but let's stick with Daniel for now.) Certainly, human political figures can wield tremendous power and affect people's lives for good or ill, sometimes for very good or very ill. But we should not attribute to them anything like ultimate power. They are, actually—and whether they know it or not—merely pawns in someone else's chess game. We should concentrate our attention much less on the pawns and much more on the One who is moving the pieces. "Do not fear those who kill the body but cannot kill the soul; rather fear him who can destroy both soul and body in hell" (Matt 10:28 // Luke 12:4–5). The message of Daniel is largely the same as the message of Jesus. You need to figure out to whom you should direct your fear. Human rulers may seem powerful, imposing, but in reality all human rule totters on a frail foundation and will be shown to be irrelevant in the light of the rule of God.

Interpretation of Dreams

While God blessed Daniel, Shadrach, Meshach, and Abednego with "knowledge and skill in every aspect of literature and wisdom," to Daniel particularly God gave skill at interpretation of dreams (Dan 1:17). The Babylonians and other ancient near eastern cultures were also known for dream interpretation; manuals for how to decipher the meaning of dreams have appeared with the discovery of ancient libraries.[1] One of the Babylonian tales most famous to modern audiences is the *Epic of*

---

1. For an overview of the practice of dream interpretation in ancient Babylon, see Stefan M. Maul, *The Art of Divination in the Ancient Near East: Reading the Signs of Heaven and Earth* (Waco, TX: Baylor University Press, 2018). An influential manual for interpreting dreams that was written in Greek around AD 200 was

Gilgamesh—surely one of the texts that the Judean boys studied as they were taught Babylonian literature (Dan 1:4)—and it features dreams prominently: Gilgamesh dreamed of Enkidu before meeting him (tablet 1), and he dreamed five times of defeating the monster Humbaba (tablet 4), and later Enkidu himself had a prophetic dream (tablet 6). So it's not really surprising that the Babylonian king would have a dream and think it was significant. But what did the dream mean?

Nebuchadnezzar summoned his magicians, enchanters, sorcerers, and Chaldeans (2:2) and demanded that they tell him his dream (2:1–11). This is a different approach from the way Pharaoh treated his magicians back in the days of Joseph; Pharaoh narrated his dream and asked for an interpretation (Gen 41:8), which only Joseph provided, though he attributed dream interpretation to God (Gen 41:16). Why does Nebuchadnezzar want his magicians (etc.) to tell him his dream first? On the one hand, it's possible that this tactic was a test of his magicians' abilities: Nebuchadnezzar perhaps wanted to know whether the magicians really had any special powers about them, or whether they were just making stuff up. On the other hand, Nebuchadnezzar may not have remembered his dream (as Josephus asserts).[2] We have often experienced this, haven't we? We wake up and remember having a dream that made us feel anxious, but we can't remember what exactly happened. This is the way Jerome put it in his Latin commentary written at the beginning of the fifth century AD:

> There remained in the king's heart only a shadow, so to speak, or a mere echo or trace of the dream, with the result that if others should tell it to him, he would be able to recall what he

Artemidorus, *The Interpretation of Dreams*, trans. Martin Hammond, Oxford World's Classics (Oxford: Oxford University Press, 2020).
2. Josephus, *Antiquities of the Jews* 10.195.

had seen, and they would certainly not be deceiving him with lies.[3]

At any rate, the wise men come close to admitting that they have no special powers: they tell their king that "no one can reveal it to the king except the gods" (Dan 2:11), and the gods aren't talking. In this exchange with the king, these wise men remind me of Professor Marvel from *The Wizard of Oz*, the fortune teller near the beginning of the movie who is able to tell Dorothy all about herself by sneaking a peak at her belongings while her eyes are closed. Professor Marvel wouldn't have been able to tell Nebuchadnezzar his dream, either.

Daniel more-or-less agrees with the Babylonian magicians: only a divine power can do what Nebuchadnezzar demands. His approach to the problem was prayer (2:17–19), and then he praised God for revealing the dream and its interpretation (2:20–23), and—like Joseph—he publicly acknowledged that the revelation of the mystery is owing to God and not to himself (2:27–30).

The Dream and Its Interpretation

Nebuchadnezzar dreamed of a strange statue made from a variety of materials with a very unstable foundation, "partly of iron and partly of clay" (2:33). (This is where the expression "feet of clay" comes from.) And then the statue was crushed by "a stone cut out, not by human hands" (2:34). The statue didn't just topple over, like Goliath; rather, it disintegrated. All the broken pieces "became like chaff ... and the wind carried them away, so that not a trace of them could be found" (2:35). If I may be permitted another *Wizard of Oz* reference, remember what happens when Dorothy throws water on the Wicked Witch of

---

3. Jerome, *Commentary on Daniel*, trans. Gleason L. Archer (Grand Rapids: Baker, 1958), 25, commenting on Daniel 2:3. This line of approach is also taken by Christopher J. H. Wright, *Hearing the Message of Daniel: Sustaining Faith in Today's World* (Downers Grove, IL: IVP, 2017), 43.

the West? In place of the statue, that stone uncut by human hands became an enormous mountain (2:35).

We can understand why Nebuchadnezzar would be disturbed by such a dream. What does it all mean? Daniel explains (2:36–45): Nebuchadnezzar's kingdom is represented by the head of gold (2:37), to be followed by an inferior kingdom of silver, and a third of bronze (2:39), and then a fourth kingdom, represented by the iron and clay (2:40–43).[4] Daniel spends more time on this fourth kingdom than on the other three, as it seems to be especially fierce: "just as iron crushes and smashes everything, it [= the fourth kingdom] shall crush and shatter all these [= the previous kingdoms?]" (2:40). But the fierceness of this fourth kingdom is not the full story, for two reasons: (1) the iron is mixed with clay, and (2) it's going to get a taste of its own medicine, since it's also about to get crushed.

Without thinking right now about the details of this statue, let's try to get an overall picture of the dream and its meaning. The statue represents human kingdoms. The statue has a head of gold and feet with an iron-clay mix, which—as Daniel says—don't actually mix (2:43). The statue looks good on top, but if you look at its foundation, you'll see that it's very unstable. There's no way that this statue is going to be able to stand very long, not with a foundation like that. And since the statue represents human kingdoms, at least part of the message would seem to be that human kingdoms are, by their very nature, unstable, subject to decay, impressive at the beginning (head of gold) but they always topple over because of their precarious foundation. As the ancient Jewish sage Sirach put it, "Sovereignty passes from

---

4. In Plato's *Republic*, Socrates also mentions people made with gold, silver, bronze, and iron (3.415a–c), and the injudicious combination of these people produces "unlikeness and discordant inequality. And when you get those, wherever they occur, they always breed war and hostility" (8.547a); trans. Tom Griffith in Plato, *The Republic*, ed. G. R. F. Ferrari (Cambridge: Cambridge University Press, 2000), 256.

nation to nation on account of injustice and insolence and wealth" (Sirach 10:8).

And the other major element of the dream is the rock that becomes a mountain, but not before destroying the statue, the representation of human kingdoms. This rock-become-mountain represents God's kingdom, which will not suffer the same fate as the human kingdoms; it "shall never be destroyed" (2:44). Moreover, "it shall crush all these kingdoms and bring them to an end." Human rule is replaced by God's rule.

The main point is that Nebuchadnezzar is not in control. He may be the head of gold, but he was put there by "the God of heaven" (2:37). Human kingdoms will come to an end, and God's kingdom will be all in all.

What Are the Kingdoms?

I'm not sure it really matters which four kingdoms the statue represents with its four metals. I'm not sure we're supposed to take guesses at which was the silver kingdom, and which was the bronze, and which the iron-clay kingdom. I think the point is probably not about identifying the human kingdoms intended by the statue and thereby predicting the timing of the kingdom of God, but rather perceiving that human kingdoms succeed one another, humans often interpret the days we're living in as worse than a bygone era (and thus the metals of the statue decrease in value), and that God's kingdom will render all human kingdoms irrelevant. I suspect that the same point would be made if the statue had five or six or seven sections, or only three. In other words, "four" is not really the point of the dream.

My view is a minority view. Most interpreters throughout the ages, and still today, want to identify the four kingdoms. Daniel 7 is also relevant here since it has a vision of four beasts, which also correspond to four kingdoms, and everybody admits that whatever the four kingdoms represent in Daniel 2, they are the same in Daniel 7.

Other ancient historians had an idea that kingdom succeeded kingdom; the concept is not original with Daniel. At the end of this chapter, I've collected some of those comments. The eighth-century BC Greek poet Hesiod already wrote about declining ages of humanity.

The traditional view is that the kingdoms in Daniel 2 are Babylon, Medo-Persia, Macedonia (Alexander the Great), and Rome. The idea that Rome is the fourth kingdom works well with a particular view of the establishment of God's kingdom "in the days of those kings" (2:44). If you identify God's kingdom with the church, and the church was established in the days of the Roman empire, then the fourth kingdom is Rome. On the other hand, another ancient view that is favored by most modern scholars is that the four kingdoms are Babylon, Media, Persia, and Macedonia.[5] This sequence would agree with the sequence of kingdoms in some other ancient sources (see the end of this chapter), and the book of Daniel in some other places definitely shows a marked interest in the kingdom of the Macedonians, e.g., all the stuff about the "king of the north" and the "king of the south" in Daniel 11.

To reiterate, I think these interpretations might be pressing the details too far. Daniel clearly uses the number "four" in a symbolic way in other chapters to express a meaning like "totality," and he might be doing the same thing with the number of kingdoms in chapters 2 and 7.[6] It makes sense to me to say that the dream indicates that in the midst of unstable human rule, God will establish His kingdom.

---

5. See discussion in Carol A. Newsom and Brennan W. Breed, *Daniel*, Old Testament Library (Louisville: WJK, 2014), including the discussion of the history of interpretation by Brennan Breed in the same commentary.
6. On the number four signifying totality, see Newsom and Breed, *Daniel*, 221, on the four winds of Daniel 7:2; and p. 224, on the four heads and four wings on the leopard of Daniel 7:6.

God's Kingdom

> And in the days of those kings the God of heaven will set up a
> kingdom that shall never be destroyed, nor shall this kingdom
> be left to another people. It shall crush all these kingdoms and
> bring them to an end, and it shall stand forever (Dan 2:44).

God will establish His kingdom. This is an extremely important
passage for understanding the New Testament. Remember
Jesus's basic message: "Repent, for the kingdom of heaven has
come near" (Matt 4:17). Jesus came to establish God's kingdom
in fulfillment of Daniel 2:44 and other prophecies. We also
remember that Jesus had little success in convincing people of
the type of kingdom He was inaugurating. Daniel 2:44 helps
explain why. According to Nebuchadnezzar's dream, the
kingdom of God would demolish the human kingdoms—especially the fourth kingdom. If that fourth kingdom is Rome—and
we have Jewish literature shortly after the time of Jesus that
makes that identification explicit[7]—then the one inaugurating
God's kingdom should make war against Rome, should crush the
fourth kingdom, turn it into chaff and scatter it to the four
winds. That is not what Jesus was going to do.

Jesus did establish a kingdom, His church. We in churches of
Christ have probably made that identification too tightly, but I
do think it is the New Testament message that the church
comprises the group of people over whom God reigns as king,
and so it is closely related to God's kingdom.[8] We could say that

---

7. 4 Ezra 12:11; Josephus, *Antiquities of the Jews* 10.209, with the commentary of
Christopher T. Begg and Paul Spilsbury, in *Flavius Josephus: Translation and
Commentary*, vol. 5: *Judean Antiquities Books 8–10* (Leiden: Brill, 2005), 282–83. See
also *Antiquities* 10.276; 15.385–87.
8. For more of my thoughts on the relationship between the church and the
kingdom of God, see the essay called "The Kingdom of God" in *Approaching
Christian Scripture Faithfully: Twenty Attempts* (Florence, AL: Heritage Christian
University Press, 2023), 154–60.

Daniel 2:44 was fulfilled when the church was established on the Day of Pentecost in Acts 2 (and I have heard many a sermon make that exact point). I won't dispute that idea.

We should notice that Daniel 2:44 has not yet been literally fulfilled. The kingdoms of the world still persist. They have not all been turned into chaff to be blown by the wind. (Maybe you'll want to say that Rome, the fourth kingdom, has been destroyed, but [I would respond] that it took hundreds of years after the death of Jesus for Rome to be succeeded by other kingdoms.) So either we should think of Daniel 2:44 as only partially fulfilled as yet, or completely fulfilled in a not-obvious way.

I myself favor the view that the outcome of Nebuchadnezzar's dream is not that kingdoms of the world will actually be destroyed by God's kingdom but rather that they will be rendered irrelevant—at least, irrelevant in a particular sense: they will be shown to be not the ultimate sources of power. We can already see that when the statue is still standing: each kingdom gives way to the next, and they all stand on an unstable foundation. Only God's kingdom endures. Whereas the dream makes one think that God's kingdom succeeds and replaces all human kingdoms, we might actually look at it as if God's kingdom "crushes" the human kingdoms in the sense that its simultaneous existence alongside the never-ending succession of human kingdoms shows that only God's kingdom is permanent. (Think: Matt 16:18.)

By the way, if the previous paragraph captures a truth about this dream, then it may imply—again—that the identity of the four kingdoms is irrelevant. If the kingdom of God exists alongside irrelevant human kingdoms, then the point of the dream may not be to predict a time when the kingdom of God would be established but to illustrate how even in the days of Nebuchadnezzar God was already reigning alongside Nebuchadnezzar's golden but irrelevant kingdom. After all, a major aspect of God's interactions with Nebuchadnezzar is to get this pagan king to recognize "that Heaven is sovereign" (4:26). And it does turn out that in chapter 4 Nebuchadnezzar praises "the King of heaven," just as later another ruler of Babylon, Darius the Mede, will recognize that already in his day Daniel's God has a kingdom that will never be destroyed (6:26). From the perspective of Daniel and Babylon, the kingdom of God is not only future but already present.

* * *

Exploration 2.1: Greek Sources on the Succession of Ages/Kingdoms

Hesiod, *Works and Days*, on the succession of ages (summary): The Olympian gods first made a golden race (lines 109–26); then a silver one, "much worse" (127–42); then a third race, of bronze (143–55)—"terrible and strong they were, and they cared only for the painful works of Ares and for acts of violence" (lines 145–55) —followed by a fourth race, "more just and superior" (156–73), the generation of the Trojan War; and now a fifth race, in the time of Hesiod himself, a race of iron (174–201).[9] The successive races are not necessarily progressively worse. The fourth race seems better than the second race but not as good as the first race.

Polybius, an eyewitness, describes the scene when the Roman general Scipio Africanus the Younger destroyed the North African city of Carthage in 146 BC.

> Scipio, when he looked upon the city as it was utterly perishing and in the last throes of its complete destruction, is said to have shed tears and wept openly for his enemies. After being wrapped in thought for long, and realizing that all cities,

---

9. See the translation in Hesiod, *Theogony; Works and Days; Testimonia*, ed. and trans. Glenn W. Most, Loeb Classical Library (Cambridge, MA: Harvard University Press, 2006), 97–105.

nations, and authorities must, like men, meet their doom; that this happened to Ilium, once a prosperous city, to the empires of Assyria, Media, and Persia, the greatest of their time, and to Macedonia itself, the brilliance of which was so recent, either deliberately or the verses escaping him, he said:

> A day will come when sacred Troy shall perish,
> And Priam and his people shall be slain.
> [*Iliad* 6.448–49]

And when Polybius speaking with freedom to him, for he was his teacher, asked him what he meant by the words, they say that without any attempt at concealment, he named his own country, for which he feared when he reflected on the fate of all things human. Polybius actually heard him and recalls it in his history.[10]

Dionysius of Halicarnassus, a first-century BC historian, writing in praise of Rome:

> For if anyone turns his attention to the successive supremacies both of cities and of nations, as accounts of them have been handed down from times past, and then, surveying them severally and comparing them together, wishes to determine which of them obtained the widest dominion and both in peace and war performed the most brilliant achievements, he will find that the supremacy of the Romans has far surpassed all those that are recorded from earlier times, not only in the extent of it dominion and in the splendour of its achievements—which no account has as yet worthily celebrated—but also in the length of time during which it has endured down to our day. (2) For the

---

10. This is book 38, §22 of Polybius' *Histories*, according to the translation of Polybius, *The Histories*, trans. W. R. Paton, vol. 6, Loeb Classical Library (Cambridge, MA: Harvard University Press, 1927), 439. This section of Polybius' work is preserved in the work of the second-century AD historian Appian, *Roman History* 8.132, for which see Appian, *Roman History*, ed. and trans. Brian McGing, vol. 2, Loeb Classical Library (Cambridge, MA: Harvard University Press, 2019), 243–45.

empire of the Assyrians, ancient as it was and running back to legendary times, held sway over only a small part of Asia. That of the Medes, after overthrowing the Assyrian empire and obtaining a still wider dominion, did not hold it long, but was overthrown in the fourth generation. The Persians, who conquered the Medes, did, indeed, finally become masters of almost all Asia; but when they attacked the nations of Europe also, they did not reduce many of them to submission, and they continued in power not much above two hundred years. (3) The Macedonian dominion, which overthrew the might of the Persians, did, in the extent of its sway, exceed all its predecessors, yet even it did not flourish long, but after Alexander's death began to decline; for it was immediately partitioned among many commanders from the time of the Diadochi, and although after their time it was able to go on to the second or third generation, yet it was weakened by its own dissensions and at the last destroyed by the Romans. (4) But even the Macedonian power did not subjugate every country and every sea; for it neither conquered Libya, with the exception of the small portion bordering on Egypt, nor subdued all Europe, but in the North advanced only as far as Thrace and in the West down to the Adriatic Sea.[11]

In a similar passage, the second-century AD Greek historian Appian compares Rome to its imperial predecessors.

Again, the duration of the Assyrians, Medes, and Persians taken together (the three greatest empires before Alexander), does not amount to nine hundred years, a period which that of Rome has already reached, and the size of their empire, I think, was not half that of the Romans, whose boundaries extend from the

---

11. This is book 1, §2.2–4 of Dionysius of Halicarnassus in the translation of Dionysius of Halicarnassus, *Roman Antiquities, Book I–II*, trans. Earnest Cary, Loeb Classical Library (Cambridge, MA: Harvard University Press, 1937), 7–9.

setting of the sun and the Western ocean to Mount Caucasus and the river Euphrates, and through Egypt up country to Ethiopia and through Arabia as far as the Eastern ocean, so that their boundary is the ocean both where the sun-god rises and where he sinks, while they control the entire Mediterranean, and all its islands as well as Britain in the ocean. But the greatest sea-power of the Medes and Persians included only the gulf of Pamphylia and the single island of Cyprus or perhaps some other small islets belonging to Ionia in the Mediterranean.[12]

In the next paragraph, Appian praises Alexander's achievements but notes that they were short-lived.

Conclusion

How does Daniel reorient our view of politics? By reminding us that human kingdoms come and go, but God's kingdom endures forever. That fact ought to have some say in our priorities, how we organize our time, to what we give our money, where we set our hopes, what we talk about with our friends, how we represent ourselves to others. Do people know us as more concerned about human kingdoms or more concerned about God's kingdom? (I have heard it said that some Christians have their thinking shaped more by cable news than by Scripture—a fact, if true, that calls into question their commitment to Jesus and calls for serious introspection and a change of behavior.) Daniel's understanding of who was in control of world history determined how he lived.

---

12. This is §9 of the Preface to Appian's history in the translation of Appian, *Roman History*, vol. 1, trans. Horace White, Loeb Classical Library (Cambridge, MA: Harvard University Press, 1912), 15.

Discussion Questions

- Compare Nebuchadnezzar's demands in Daniel 2:1–12 with the similar story about Pharaoh at Genesis 41:1–8. Why does Nebuchadnezzar demand for the wise men to tell him the dream? What are the implications of what the wise men say at Daniel 2:11? See Genesis 41:16.
- What does Daniel do between hearing about the death sentence for wise men (Dan 2:13) and announcing that he would supply the king's requested interpretation (2:24)?
- ·Nebuchadnezzar dreamed about a statue (Dan 2:31–35). In his dream, what happened to the statue?
- According to Daniel, what does the statue represent?
- According to Daniel, what is represented by the stone cut out not by human hands?

Chapter 3
In the Fiery Furnace

You shall not make for yourself an idol, whether in the form of anything that is in heaven above, or that is on the earth beneath, or that is in the water under the earth. You shall not bow down to them or worship them; for I YHWH your God am a jealous God, punishing children for the iniquity of parents, to the third and the fourth generation of those who reject me, but showing steadfast love to the thousandth generation of those who love me and keep my commandments (Exod 20:4–6).

How easy it is to worship idols, to convince ourselves that God doesn't mind, or that He wouldn't really expect us to stand against an entire culture! Idolatry is all around us, in a slightly less conspicuous way than it was in the ancient Near East, or in ancient Greece and Rome, or in many modern nations. In the West, we have renamed our idols so that it becomes a little less obvious how we have betrayed the faith we confess. Of course, Jesus isn't buying it. He recognizes that many people serve Mammon alongside God, which is, as He tells us, an impossible task (Matt 16:24). Jesus didn't actually use the word idolatry, but Paul did (Col 3:5). And if greed can be considered a form of idolatry because it divides our loyalties, then so can all kinds of other things: career, social status, political correctness, social media, entertainment, houses, cars, food, sex, sports. The fact that we don't call these things idols makes the sin all the harder to recognize. The fact that each of these things is perfectly innocuous in moderation and in the right circumstances makes the idolatry all the more insidious.

On second thought, sometimes our idols are named as such. There's a TV show called *American Idol*.

In Daniel 3, Shadrach, Meshach, and Abednego are confronted with an idol—not an inconspicuous idol, but one very much larger than life, easy to recognize. It was made of gold, and it was sixty cubits tall (= about 90 feet) and six cubits wide (= about nine feet). For comparison, the statue of a sitting Abraham Lincoln in the Lincoln Memorial in Washington, DC, is 19 feet tall, and the building itself is 99 feet tall. I suppose a statue in and of itself wouldn't be an idol; we have statues all over the place that we don't regard as idols. But Nebuchadnezzar wanted his subjects "to fall down and worship" the statue (Dan 3:5). And the people did just as Nebuchadnezzar demanded: they "fell down and worshiped the golden statue that King Nebuchadnezzar had set up" (3:7). They all like sheep have gone astray (Isa 53:6). They have drunk the Kool-Aid.

The Resistance

Well, not everybody. Three Jewish boys refused. Now, presumably, Daniel didn't fall down in front of the statue, either, but this chapter does not mention Daniel at all. It focuses on Daniel's friends, Shadrach, Meshach, and Abednego. We have been briefly introduced to these friends in the first two chapters, in stories that focus mostly on Daniel. After Daniel 3, the focus shifts back to Daniel, and Shadrach, Meshach, and Abednego are never mentioned again. Before they exit stage left, we have one powerful story demonstrating their total allegiance to God.

Let's not kid ourselves: even though these Jewish boys are

being told to perform what is obviously a sin, it must have been difficult for them to decide what to do. None of that difficulty is reflected in this chapter, which shows the boys resolved to disobey the king. But we can guess at this difficulty because we are humans, and it would probably be difficult for us. Everybody else is doing it, apparently without any scruples. Refusing would mean certain death (unless God intervenes, as the boys are hoping). Wouldn't we do a better job of testifying to our God by staying alive rather than by dying? Is it really idolatry to bow down to this statue? Isn't it really the heart that matters, so if we're not inwardly bowing down to the statue, but only doing so outwardly, maybe it doesn't really count? Or, to give a somewhat more recent example, imagine being told on Kristallnacht to throw a brick through the window of a Jewish owned business, lest your own loyalty to the regime come into doubt.

My guess is that most of us would have a very hard time figuring out what to do, which is why we need stories like Daniel 3 (and Daniel 6, another near-martyrdom story).

Nebuchadnezzar confronts these boys and gives his command directly to them (3:13–15), in a speech that ends with the rhetorical question: "Who is the god that will deliver you out of my hands?" I love Jerome's imagined response to this question: "Why naturally, that same God whose servant you recently worshiped and whom you asserted to be truly God of gods and Lord of kings" (Dan 2:46–47).[1] Maybe Nebuchadnezzar is thinking that revealing secrets (Dan 2) is one thing, but delivering from a fiery furnace is something altogether different.[2]

The boys do not hesitate:

Shadrach, Meshach, and Abednego answered and said to the

---

1. This is Jerome's comment on Dan 3:15 in his early-fifth-century *Commentary on Daniel*, trans. Gleason L. Archer (Grand Rapids: Baker, 1958), 37 (translation slightly adapted).

2. Nebuchadnezzar's method of killing by a furnace had become well-known among the Jewish exiles (cf. Jer 29:21–22).

king, "O Nebuchadnezzar, we have no need to answer you in
this matter. If this be so, our God whom we serve is able to
deliver us from the burning fiery furnace, and he will deliver us
out of your hand, O king. But if not, be it known to you, O
king, that we will not serve your gods or worship the golden
image that you have set up." (Dan 3:16–18)[3]

The highlight here is "but if not." The boys have confidence
in their God, but they don't have complete confidence in their
ability to predict what God will do. He can save us, but sometimes He chooses not to, for whatever reason. In this context,
we might remember the prayer of Paul that God would remove
the thorn in his flesh, only to be told, "My grace is sufficient for
you, for power is made perfect in weakness" (2 Cor 12:9). Or,
even more relevant, we recall the prayer of Jesus that the Father
would "take this cup from me, yet not as I will, but as you will"
(Mark 14:36). We remember the outcome of that prayer: the
Father did not remove the cup. Jesus tells His followers to take
up their own crosses (Mark 8:34).

The boys' response to Nebuchadnezzar might also remind us
of this other statement from Jesus when He was facing certain
death: "You would have no power over me if it were not given
you from above" (John 19:11).

Probably in a reflection on this story in Daniel 3, another
ancient Jewish document (4 Maccabees, written in the first
century AD) puts these words into the mouth of a Jew facing the
choice of death or apostasy: "You do not have a fire hot enough
to make me play the coward" (4 Macc 10:14). Later, he encouraged others: "Let us imitate the three youths in Assyria who
despised the same ordeal of the furnace" (13:9).

---

3. The translation of verse 17 is problematic, with various renderings. See the
discussion in John J. Collins, *Daniel*, Hermeneia (Minneapolis: Fortress, 1993),
187–88.

In the Furnace[4]

God does save the boys, after all. Some sort of supernatural person joins the boys in the furnace, one that seemed to Nebuchadnezzar to have "the appearance of a son of the gods" (Dan 3:25), while the king later calls this fourth person an angel (3:28). Who was it? The text does not say. Or, at least the Aramaic text does not say; the Septuagint (Old Greek and Theodotion) specifies that it was "an angel of the Lord."[5] Of course, "angel of the Lord" could be considered one of the titles of Jesus, and indeed in early Christianity, it was common to identify this fourth person as the pre-incarnate Christ. It would be difficult to argue against that interpretation, but it would also be difficult to know for sure. In the fourth century AD, Jerome expressed some doubts:

> As for the appearance of the fourth man, which he asserts to be like that of a son of God, either we must take him to be an angel, as the Septuagint has rendered it, or indeed, as the majority think, the Lord our Savior. Yet I do not know how an ungodly king could have merited a vision of the Son of God.[6]

In any case, this fourth person brought the salvation of God.

It might be significant to recognize that God does not intervene in this story until the last possible minute. (That aspect might remind us of Genesis 22.) Ellen Davis has helpfully

---

4. The Greek translation has a longer version of Daniel 3. After the boys are thrown into the fiery furnace, one of them (Azariah = Abednego) offers a prayer, and then all three boys sing a hymn. This additional material is found in the Greek translation between Daniel 3:23 and 3:24.

5. This identification comes in the additional part of the fiery furnace story found in the Greek (and Latin, etc.) versions and accepted as Scripture in the Roman Catholic Church (among others). The addition is called "The Prayer of Azariah and the Song of the Three Young Men," and the statement about the angel comes between the prayer and the song.

6. Jerome, *Commentary on Daniel*, trans. Archer, 43.

brought up this point: "For this particular storyteller, it is surely important that the fourth figure becomes visible only in the furnace, the locus of the most intense suffering."[7]

This story encourages us to trust God all the way, even beyond death.

Facing Martyrdom

Part of what I imagine made the boys pause when they initially heard the command about bowing down to the statue is the suddenness of the change in Babylonian policy. Shadrach, Meshach, and Abednego had been able to carve out a pretty comfortable existence even in exile. They were honored along with Daniel as wise men, wiser than others, experts in Babylonian literature. And Nebuchadnezzar had seemed open to their practicing their religion however they chose. Then the king makes a new law, one that must have seemed to him rather innocent, encouraging loyalty among the diverse population of his empire. That's the line the Judean boys can't cross.

The resolve of these boys had been made easier, no doubt, by their earlier stand in regard to the luxurious foods of Babylon. They had already refused to become completely assimilated to their new culture; they had already resolved to maintain their distinctiveness; they had already determined that they needed to hold Babylon at arm's length. And so when the shock of this new command came to them, they had trained themselves to face the challenge.

You've seen clips of the Nazi-propaganda film *Triumph of the Will*. I doubt you've endured watching the whole thing. You can find it online, and it is generally considered one of the greatest documentaries ever made (but an evil one!), but you can probably hold that opinion only if you don't watch it. That's exactly

7. Ellen F. Davis, *Opening Israel's Scriptures* (Oxford: Oxford University Press, 2019), 390.

the position Roger Ebert found himself in a few years before his death, after decades of supposing that everyone knew what they were talking about when they acclaimed this film as so great. Upon watching it in his older age, Ebert wrote: "It is a terrible film, paralyzingly dull, simpleminded, overlong and not even 'manipulative,' because it is too clumsy to manipulate anyone but a true believer."[8] So I am not recommending the film to you—not because I think it will make you a Nazi, but because it's a boring film. But, the reason I wanted to bring up the film is that it documents a rather sudden shift in German society.[9] The film focuses on a pro-Hitler rally in 1934. Remember, Hitler had become German chancellor in 1933, so this is just a little bit later. But the people worship Hitler. Pastor Julius Leutheuser exclaimed: "Christ has come to us through Adolf Hitler. Through his power, his honesty, his faith and his idealism ... the Redeemer has found us, [and] we know the Savior today has come!"[10] That's the twentieth century.

Now, in the twenty-first century in America, how much would our country have to change for it to require of us things that Shadrach, Meshach, and Abednego were not willing to do? Maybe it's already there? Maybe it's not? In any case, change can come suddenly. Are we ready to imitate these boys?

They got themselves ready by training themselves to resist the empire's allures. Perhaps we should think of ways to do this, as well. Sometimes we say, "Well, if you were in the situation in Daniel 3, you don't know how you would respond. You really don't know until you're in that situation." That may be true to some extent, but we can train ourselves. After all, we don't

---

8. You can find Ebert's review on his website, https://www.rogerebert.com/.

9. For a very readable account of this shift in German society, see Erik Larson, *In the Garden of Beasts: Love, Terror, and an American Family in Hitler's Berlin* (New York: Crown, 2011).

10. See J. S. Conway, *The Nazi Persecution of the Churches 1933–1945* (Vancouver: Regent College Publishing, 1968), 48. I originally found this quotation in Charles Marsh, *Strange Glory: A Life of Dietrich Bonhoeffer* (New York: Knopf, 2014), 176.

accept such excuses from our military. It's not like an army general ever tells the President, "We can send troops into this area, but we really don't know how they'll respond, because they've never been in that situation." True, some soldiers will get into a tense situation and react through fear rather than in accordance with their training, but the point of the training is to minimize that response.

Listen to John Chrysostom's encouragement to his fourth-century audience at the conclusion of one of his sermons on the martyrs. After exhorting his hearers to imitate those believers who willingly and boldly gave their lives for their faith, Chrysostom says that Christians need to prepare themselves

> by conquering the passions in us before the wars and tortures in this time of peace, by pruning the undisciplined stirrings of the flesh, by mortifying the body and treating it as a slave. For if we live our life in this fashion in a time of peace, we shall receive brilliant crowns for our training. If God who loves humankind decides to effect the same contest for us, we shall come to the wrestling matches prepared and shall attain the heavenly blessings.[11]

We need training to hold the earthly kingdoms at arm's length. The New Testament repeatedly encourages us to be prepared for suffering (Acts 14:22; Phil 1:27–30; 2 Tim 3:12; 1 Pet 4:1–2). Our danger in twenty-first-century America is that we have become so accustomed to comfort, we have become so unfamiliar with suffering, that we misinterpret our society and suffering, and we think that the prospect of the loss of our church's tax-exempt status is persecution. Of course, we should by all means be willing to forgo our tax-exempt status, but

---

11. John Chrysostom, *Homily 2 on the Maccabees* §6, in St John Chrysostom, *The Cult of the Saints*, trans. Wendy Mayer and Bronwen Neil (Crestwood, NY: St Vladimir's Seminary Press, 2006), 153. I have removed brackets in the translation for readability.

Shadrach, Meshach, and Abednego were willing to do a great deal more than that. And so are many other Christians around the world today. Just do an online search for modern Christian martyrdom, and you'll find that it's on the rise.

Daniel 3 reminds us of the commitment we have made to take up our cross, which we sometimes sing about.

> *Our fathers, chained in prisons dark,*
> *Were still in heart and conscience free;*
> *And blest would be their children's fate,*
> *If they, like them should die for thee:*
> *Faith of our fathers! holy faith!*
> *We will be true to thee till death!*

Or, in the words of our Lord: "Be faithful unto death, and I will give you a crown of life" (Rev 2:10).

Discussion Questions

- As you read through Daniel 3, do you think that Nebuchadnezzar changes? How does he change?
- What is Nebuchadnezzar's new plan in Daniel 3:1–7? Why does he make such a plan?
- Why do the Chaldeans behave as they do (Dan 3:8–12)? Have the events of Daniel 2 influenced the Chaldeans?
- How do Shadrach, Meshach, and Abednego respond to the king's demand? Can you think of examples in the modern period of people doing similar things: acting with courage and piety in the face of certain death?
- What means does God use to save Shadrach, Meshach, and Abednego? How does the salvation in Daniel 3 compare to the story of Christian salvation?

Chapter 4
The Madness of King Nebuchadnezzar

Is this not magnificent Babylon, which I have built as a royal capital by my mighty power and for my glorious majesty? (Dan 4:30)

These are the words of Nebuchadnezzar, and two things immediately pop into mind when I read them: (1) he shouldn't have said that! These words are the turning point in the story, and they lead to the situation depicted in the painting *Nebuchadnezzar* by William Blake, c. 1795, which is definitely worth googling. (2) His words sound really familiar, like things I have said any number of times.

Because, you know, I think pretty highly of myself. I've been able to accomplish some amazing things in my life, and I've got a ways to go, yet—I'm not that old. I'm only going to become more impressive. "Is not this a magnificent career—and family, and reputation, and Christian service—that I have built by my mighty power and for my glorious majesty?"

I need Daniel 4. Probably a lot of us do. This story shows how ridiculous God thinks it is when we talk about our lives as if we have accomplished wonderful things. Because we haven't. Yeah, Babylon might be impressive, and Nebuchadnezzar might have been in charge during its glory days, but only because God set him on the throne. I mean, that is what Daniel has already told him: "You, O king, the king of kings—to whom the God of heaven has given the kingdom" (Dan 2:37). Anything I have ever accomplished, I didn't really accomplish so much as God accomplished it through me. I didn't cause myself to exist. I don't provide air for my lungs. I don't oversee the beating of my heart or the functioning of my brain. I don't even understand any of this stuff. What I ought to reflect on, instead of thinking about how wonderful I am, is the truth spoken by an itinerant teacher in Athens in the middle of the first century; speaking about God, this teacher told the assembled philosophers in the audience: "In him we live and move and have our being" (Acts 17:28).

This is about humility, about which the Bible has a lot to say. Let me cite here just a couple of famous verses.

> Humble yourselves before the Lord, and he will exalt you (Jas 4:10).

> The last will be first, and the first will be last (Matt 20:16).

Nebuchadnezzar's Last Chapter

We've had three chapters in which King Nebuchadnezzar features as one of the chief characters. (Well, chapter 1, not so much, but he does appear in that chapter.) Daniel 4 is the last one in which Nebuchadnezzar appears. His name is mentioned in Daniel 5 as the father of the reigning king Belshazzar, and that's it; no more Nebuchadnezzar in Daniel after that.

This chapter is unique in that it is narrated in the first person from the perspective of Nebuchadnezzar himself. The king is telling this story. The chapter is set up like a royal proclamation: the king has an announcement to make to his kingdom. What he wants to say is in praise of the Most High God. This is how he begins (4:2-3) and ends (4:34-37). The king has fully experienced the power of the Most High God, and he knows what he's talking about when he concludes the chapter by saying that the King of heaven "is able to bring low those who walk in pride" (4:37).

In this story, Nebuchadnezzar again has a dream, just like in chapter 2. This time he has no hesitation about narrating the dream to his magicians (4:7); he does not demand that they tell the dream to him (as at 2:5–9). Even so, the magicians can't provide any help. They have no idea what the dream means, so in comes Daniel.[1]

The dream (4:10–17): A big tree gets chopped down. That's the basic plot of the dream. But there are some weird elements, also. The stump of the tree is left, and its mind—yes, the mind of the tree stump—is changed "from that of a human," and the command is given, "let the mind of an animal be given to it [or him]" (4:16). This change is going to last for "seven times"—or, as the Septuagint (Old Greek) says, "seven years" (4:16, 32, 33–34). The command to chop down the tree and switch out the mind of the tree stump for an animal's mind is said to be a decree of the "watchers," which is a type of angel. And the point? "That all who live may know that the Most High is sovereign over the kingdom of mortals; he gives it to whom he will and sets over it the lowliest of human beings" (4:17).

All of that is in the dream itself. No interpretation necessary. This is the stuff that Nebuchadnezzar tells Daniel. We might think that the meaning of the dream is so obvious as to hardly need interpretation, certainly not divine revelation. But Nebuchadnezzar seems not to get it. And since this chapter is teaching us about humility, we should probably admit that were

---

1. The Greek historian Herodotus tells of some more-or-less contemporary events in the kingdom of Media when the king Astyages has some dreams that are interpreted by magi. Astyages is satisfied with the interpretation, until the advice from the magi proves incorrect, whereupon he impales them. See Herodotus *Histories*, 1.106–28. Later, Cyrus of Persia had a dream that he interpreted himself, but incorrectly (1.209–10).

we in his situation, we would probably also be resistant to the dream's lesson and seek out clarification.

Daniel interprets: the tree is Nebuchadnezzar (4:22).

> You shall be driven away from human society, and your dwelling shall be with the wild animals. You shall be made to eat grass like oxen, you shall be bathed with the dew of heaven, and seven times shall pass over you, until you have learned that the Most High has sovereignty over the kingdom of mortals, and gives it to whom he will (4:25).

Notice that Daniel repeats the point already expressed in the dream: the Most High is in control, not any person. The Most High dispenses dominion according to His own pleasure (4:17, 25). It would be improper for any king to take pride in his own accomplishments since he is merely God's servant.

This same lesson is given in other parts of Scripture, even in reference to this same king. Let's listen to Jeremiah.

> Thus says YHWH of hosts, the God of Israel: This is what you shall say to your masters: It is I who by my great power and my outstretched arm have made the earth, with the people and animals that are on the earth, and I give it to whomever I please. Now I have given all these lands into the hand of King Nebuchadnezzar of Babylon, my servant, and I have given him even the wild animals of the field to serve him. All the nations shall serve him and his son and his grandson, until the time of his own land comes; then many nations and great kings shall make him their slave (Jer 27:4–7).

Now, the message of Jeremiah is different from that of Daniel. Jeremiah needed to tell other people that they should serve Nebuchadnezzar or face punishment from God (Jer 24:8). But the point God makes in Daniel 4 could also be derived from this passage in Jeremiah. God controls the kingdoms of men.

Nebuchadnezzar is in charge because God put him there. He will continue to be in charge as long as God wants him there. Eventually, God will make a change. That was the point of Nebuchadnezzar's dream of the statue in chapter 2. That's the point of Nebuchadnezzar's dream in chapter 4.

* * *

Exploration 4.1 The Hanging Garden in Babylon?

Part of the glory of Babylon was the legendary Hanging Garden, one of the Seven Wonders of the Ancient World. We don't have good, contemporary evidence for the Hanging Garden. The first-century Jewish historian Josephus attributes the construction of the Hanging Garden to Nebuchadnezzar himself, but I believe he is the only source who says that Nebuchadnezzar built the Garden. An earlier source, Diodorus Siculus, does not name Nebuchadnezzar, but his account might be consistent with Nebuchadnezzar's having built the Garden. At any rate, it is not at all clear who built the Garden or where it was located.[2] I bring it up here because it is a legendary feature of Babylon's beauty traditionally ascribed to Nebuchadnezzar, and so therefore it might help us think about how people thought about his Babylon and the sorts of things he might have been reflecting on when he considered his magnificent city.

Diodorus Siculus (first century BC) on the Hanging Garden.[3]

There was also, beside the acropolis, the Hanging Garden, as it is called [ὁ κρεμαστὸς καλούμενος κῆπος], which was built, not by Semiramis, but by a later Syrian king to please one of his

---

2. For a scholarly but accessible investigation, see Stephanie Dalley, *The Mystery of the Hanging Garden of Babylon: An Elusive World Wonder Traced* (Oxford: Oxford University Press, 2013).
3. Diodorus Siculus 2.10 in *The Library of History*, trans. C. H. Oldfather, Loeb Classical Library 279 (Cambridge, MA: Harvard University Press, 1933), 383–87.

concubines; for she, they say, being a Persian by race and longing
for the meadows of her mountains, asked the king to imitate,
through the artifice of a planted garden, the distinctive land-
scape of Persia. The park [ὁ παράδεισος] extended four plethra
on each side, and since the approach to the garden sloped like a
hillside and the several parts of the structure rose from one
another tier on tier, the appearance of the whole resembled that
of a theatre. When the ascending terraces had been built, there
had been constructed beneath them galleries which carried the
entire weight of the planted garden and rose little by little one
above the other along the approach; and the uppermost gallery,
which was fifty cubits high, bore the highest surface of the park,
which was made level with the circuit wall of the battlements of
the city. Furthermore, the walls, which had been constructed at
great expense, were twenty-two feet thick, while the passage-
way between each two walls was ten feet wide. The roofs of the
galleries were covered over with beams of stone sixteen feet
long, inclusive of the overlap, and four feet wide. The roof
above these beams had first a layer of reeds laid in great quanti-
ties of bitumen, over this two courses of baked brick bonded by
cement, and as a third layer a covering of lead, to the end that
the moisture from the soil might not penetrate beneath. On all
this again earth had been piled to a depth sufficient for the
roots of the largest trees; and the ground, when levelled off, was
thickly planted with trees of every kind that, by their great size
or any other charm, could give pleasure to the beholder. And
since the galleries, each projecting beyond another, all received
the light, they contained many royal lodgings of every description; and there was one gallery which contained openings
leading from the topmost surface and machines for supplying
the garden with water, the machines raising the water in great
abundance from the river, although no one outside could see it
being done. Now this park, as I have said, was a later
construction.

Josephus, *Against Apion* 1.141, quotes the third-century-BC Babylonian historian Berosus to the effect that Nebuchadnezzar

> built high stone terraces and gave them a scenery closely resembling mountains, planting them with all sorts of trees, thus constructing and landscaping the so-called 'hanging garden,' because his wife, who had been raised in the region of Media, hankered after the mountain environment.[4]

* * *

Daniel's Response

Daniel does a couple of interesting things in his response to Nebuchadnezzar. First, he makes it clear that he doesn't want Nebuchadnezzar to experience the predicted hardship. Second, he offers good advice to Nebuchadnezzar. Let's think about both of these points in turn.

When Daniel heard Nebuchadnezzar's dream, he "was severely distressed for a while. His thoughts terrified him" (4:19). He wished that the dream applied to Nebuchadnezzar's enemies rather than to the king. Is this the way you would have felt had you been in Daniel's shoes? How would you feel if the king who had taken you captive, had destroyed your nation, had tried to incinerate your friends—how would you feel if that king received some bad news? Maybe you're as pure-hearted as Daniel, but I think a few people might feel just a bit gleeful about Nebuchadnezzar's misfortune. Daniel here reminds me a little of Jesus (Luke 23:34), or Stephen (Acts 7:60), praying for the people killing him.

The advice that Daniel gives Nebuchadnezzar is also worthy of note.

---

4. Trans. John M. G. Barclay, in *Flavius Josephus: Translation and Commentary*, vol. 10: *Against Apion* (Leiden: Brill, 2007), 85.

Therefore, O king, may my counsel be acceptable to you: atone
for your sins with righteousness, and your iniquities with mercy
to the oppressed, so that your prosperity may be prolonged
(4:27).

Here we see one of the problems with Nebuchadnezzar's
pride: it resulted in the oppression of others. At least, I think
that's why Daniel gives him this advice.[5] Apparently, Nebuchadnezzar had become so impressed with himself that he failed to
perceive the deprivation outside his door. We might compare
Solomon, whose building policies produced a magnificent palace
and a beautiful temple and a very frustrated workforce (cf. 1 Kgs
12:4). Or we could think of Marie Antoinette, who apparently
did not actually say her most famous comment,[6] when told that
the people of France had no bread: "Let them eat cake!"
Nebuchadnezzar needed to stop admiring himself and take a
look around, to learn about the true, human cost for his magnificent Babylon.

The Result

The fulfillment of the dream plays out in one verse. Perhaps
Nebuchadnezzar heeded Daniel's advice for a year, but he still

---

5. On this verse, see Gary A. Anderson, *Sin: A History* (New Haven, CT: Yale
University Press, 2009), 10, and much more extensively in ch. 9 (pp. 135–51).
Anderson argues that the word translated "righteousness" actually means "alms-
giving" (as it would definitely come to mean in rabbinic literature [see Wikipedia:
Tsedakah], and as it already could mean in the Dead Sea Scrolls and even in the
Bible sometimes). He also argues that "mercy to the oppressed" in this verse is
more sensibly translated "generosity to the poor," as the Hebrew/Aramaic root
for "mercy" (*ḥnn*) can refer to generosity even in the Bible (e.g. Ps 37:21; 112:4–5;
Prov 14:21, 31; 19:17; 28:8). The parallelism in our verse between right-
eousness/almsgiving and "mercy to the oppressed" (or poor) confirms for
Anderson that Daniel advises Nebuchadnezzar to give alms to atone for his sins,
and not necessarily (as in my interpretation above) to people that he has personally deprived or oppressed. Anderson acknowledges his dependence on Franz
Rosenthal, "Ṣĕdāqâh, Charity," *Hebrew Union College Annual* 23 (1950–51): 411–30.
6. Wikipedia: "Let Them Eat Cake!"

hadn't fully learned his lesson. So he said those words of self-admiration quoted at the beginning of this lesson. And then this happened:

> Immediately the sentence was fulfilled against Nebuchadnezzar. He was driven away from human society, ate grass like oxen, and his body was bathed with the dew of heaven, until his hair grew as long as eagles' feathers and his nails became like birds' claws (4:33).

It all seems a bit odd, and some Christians in antiquity wondered whether this story about Nebuchadnezzar was not intended literally but only spiritually.[7] Then again, in the next chapter, Daniel refers to the period of Nebuchadnezzar's madness (5:20–21). There's a Dead Sea Scroll that tells a similar story about a different Babylonian king, Nabonidus.[8] I am also reminded of the *Epic of Gilgamesh*, the opening tablet of which describes the character Enkidu, who endured the opposite process of Nebuchadnezzar here, starting as a wild beast of a man and being humanized.

The point of the story seems pretty clear: Nebuchadnezzar is not in control. He's not in control of what he eats, or what he wears, or how long his fingernails are. He certainly is not in control of a kingdom, unless God says so. God is in control.

Lessons

The lessons in this one are straightforward.

---

7. See Jerome's report (and rejection) of this view in his *Commentary on Daniel*, trans. Gleason L. Archer (Grand Rapids: Baker, 1958), 46–47.

8. The *Prayer of Nabonidus*. For my take on this text, see Ed Gallagher, "Daniel and the Dead Sea Scrolls," in *Identity in Crisis: Daniel's Vision for the Future: The 81st Annual Freed-Hardeman University Lectureship*, ed. Doug Y. Burleson (Henderson, TN: Freed-Hardeman University, 2017), 410–14.

1. You're not as good as you think you are.
2. Love your neighbor.

These lessons are related, as we've already seen. The rich man in Jesus's parable (Luke 16:19–31) might well have thought that he deserved his wealth because of his hard work and intelligence, and if Lazarus would stop just sitting at the gate, maybe he'd find a job and get something to eat. "His poverty is his fault, and I deserve my wealth." Of course, that is not what Jesus thought. This story in Daniel 4 also suggests a better way of looking at life.

Let me also remind you of the movie *Groundhog Day*, which you should commit to watching once per year. Phil Connors starts out as a complete jerk, full of himself, resentful of others for not being properly impressed with him. It is a cycle that he cannot break until he stops thinking about himself, starts thinking about others. At the end of the movie, he is completely invested in others, what he can do for them, without seeking any praise for himself. You remember what Phil says to Rita after he realizes that tomorrow finally came? "Is there anything I can do for you today?" And he's happy.

Daniel 4 is not a chapter that tells us we'll be happier if we think about others more than about ourselves. It's more a chapter about how stupid it is to think that we're so great, to not realize that ultimately we control almost nothing. According to Miss Maudie Atkinson, the reason Atticus Finch doesn't take pride in his ability to shoot a gun is because it comes so easily to him. "People in their right minds never take pride in their talents."[9] Nebuchadnezzar, who marveled at the wonderful city that he had built, had surely never laid a single brick.[10] In some ways, he was the one person who was least responsible for the

---

9. This statement from Miss Maudie comes near the end of ch. 10 of Harper Lee, *To Kill a Mockingbird* (New York: HarperCollins, 1960).

10. As pointed out by Christopher J. H. Wright, *Hearing the Message of Daniel: Sustaining Faith in Today's World* (Downers Grove, IL: IVP, 2017), 101.

greatness of Babylon, but he got to enjoy most of the benefits of that greatness. That situation should have given him humility. God made sure he eventually learned the lesson.

Discussion Questions

- Why does God send Nebuchadnezzar another dream in Daniel 4? Why is God trying to communicate with this king?
- Why do you think Daniel reacts to Nebuchadnezzar's dream the way he does (4:19)? Is this reaction surprising to you?
- What kind of advice does Daniel give Nebuchadnezzar (4:27)? What does this advice imply about the type of life Nebuchadnezzar has been living?
- Why do you think twelve months passed between the dream and the fulfillment of the dream (4:28)?
- What lesson does Nebuchadnezzar learn in this chapter?

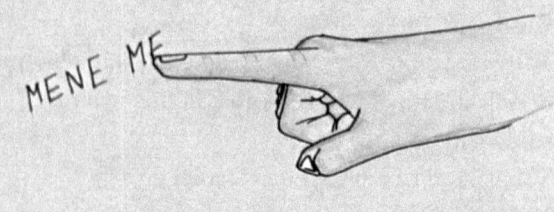

Chapter 5
The Writing on the Wall

Imagine—if you will—an entire society changing very quickly, seemingly in the blink of an eye. Imagine a government humming along, the economy performing well, abundance and prosperity (for those in power), everything going pretty much as one would hope. And then, almost without warning, everything changes. Normal life is completely interrupted—and the main point is: it all happens quickly. I don't think it will be too hard for you to imagine such a scenario, because these types of things happen relatively frequently. (I am writing this in April 2020. Do you remember what was happening then?)

That's what's happening in Daniel 5. Normal life—and then, all of a sudden, a drastic change. Within the context of Daniel 5, the problem is the stupidity of the king, doing something he shouldn't have done. God swiftly brings to an end not only this king's rule but the entire empire he ruled. We remember how patient—comparatively speaking—God had been with Nebuchadnezzar, sending him warning after warning to shape up. In Daniel 5, the new king, Belshazzar, seemingly does one dumb thing and God makes him pay. We often find, in the Bible and in our own lives, that God seems extremely, excruciatingly patient as if He will never act to bring justice—but then, in other situations, God seems to act with amazing, almost horrifying, swiftness. On the one hand, God sent prophet after prophet to Israel to admonish them to repent (cf. Amos 4:6–12; Mark 12:1–12); on the other hand, Nadab and Abihu made one wrong move (Lev 10:1–2). King Saul sinned once and was told that his dynasty would come to an end (1 Sam 13:8–14); David sinned many times and was promised an everlasting kingdom (2 Sam 7:8–16). The book of Daniel shows Nebuchadnezzar doing several stupid things and continuing to reign, while Belshazzar does one dumb thing and is killed. It seems unfair, but what can we say? God sees everything, knows everything, and we either trust Him to make the right call, or we don't. I certainly don't trust myself to decide whether God's justice is truly just.

Daniel 5 reminds us of the judgment of God. The epistle to the Hebrews tells us, "It is a terrifying thing to fall into the hands of the living God" (Heb 11:31). Daniel 5 shows us what that looks like.

The King

The previous chapter ended with Nebuchadnezzar still king of Babylon. Chapter 5 begins with someone else as king, someone named Belshazzar. Soon we are told that this is Nebuchadnezzar's son (5:2). Babylonian sources, however, mention no king named Belshazzar, but they do mention a Belshazzar who was the son of a king, but not the son of Nebuchadnezzar. The last official king of Babylon, according to Babylonian and Greek sources, was a fellow named Nabonidus, who had usurped the throne from the grandson of Nebuchadnezzar.[1] In other words, Nabonidus was not descended from Nebuchadnezzar.

---

1. Nabonidus' status as a usurper is confirmed in the Dynastic Prophecy (see: Livius.org, "Dynastic Prophecy"), and in the two extant accounts of the accession of Nabonidus: (1) Berossus (as preserved in Josephus, *Against Apion* 1.145–53) and (2) the Babylon Stela (named for the location of discovery; sometimes called the Istanbul Stela, after its current location in a museum; translated in ANET 309–

The son of Nabonidus was Belshazzar.[2] The most famous thing about Nabonidus is that he took an extended vacation during his reign and left his son in charge of Babylon.[3] So, even though Babylonian sources never call Belshazzar "king"—he is the unnamed "crown prince" in the *Nabonidus Chronicle*—he was basically the guy in charge for much of his father's reign. As a leading scholar of Nabonidus has written, "During Nabonidus' absence Belshazzar assumed the regency."[4] One ancient text even says that Nabonidus entrusted the "kingship" to his oldest son during his absence.[5] The Babylonians did not use the word "king" for Belshazzar, but we might compare the language different cultures used for the Roman emperor in the first century: for Greek speakers, the emperor was a king (*basileus*), but Latin speakers, and certainly Romans, refrained from using the word *rex* for the emperor. So, the fact that Daniel 5 calls Belshazzar "king" isn't so strange.

It's a little stranger that Daniel 5 calls Belshazzar the son of Nebuchadnezzar. He was not the biological son of Nebuchadnezzar, and probably not related to him in any way.[6] It's not hard

---

11). Moreover, the Harran Inscription of Nabonidus implies his non-royal origins (see the opening paragraph in ANET 562). ANET = *Ancient Near Eastern Texts Related to the Old Testament*, ed. James B. Pritchard, 2d ed. (Princeton: Princeton University Press, 1955).

2. Belshazzar is mentioned as Nabonidus' son in many inscriptions, such as the *Nabonidus Cylinder from Ur* (see a translation at Livius.org). See Paul-Alain Beaulieu, *The Reign of Nabonidus King of Babylon 556–539 B.C.* (New Haven: Yale University Press, 1989), 90–98, 155–60.

3. See the *Nabonidus Chronicle*, translated in ANET 305–6, or online at Livius.org; and the *Verse Account of Nabonidus* (ANET 312–15, or online at Livius.org, and at the British Museum website, for which google "British Museum 38299"). See also Beaulieu, *Reign of Nabonidus*, 149–54.

4. Beaulieu, *Reign of Nabonidus*, 185.

5. The *Verse Account of Nabonidus*. ANET 313 renders the lines: "He entrusted the 'camp' to his oldest (son), the first-born, / The troops everywhere in the country he ordered under his (command). / He let (everything) go, entrusted the kingship to him / And, himself, he started out for a long journey, / The (military) forces of Akkad marching with him; / He turned towards Tema (deep) in the west."

6. Belshazzar is called son of Nebuchadnezzar also in the apocryphal book of Baruch 1:11. Some commentators on Daniel mention the possibility that

to imagine Belshazzar as "son" of Nebuchadnezzar in some way that does not rely on biology, as in: Belshazzar is a ruler over the same empire that Nebuchadnezzar ruled.[7] After all, Nabonidus emphasized his legitimacy as king of Babylon by representing himself as a valid descendent of Nebuchadnezzar, even if the relationship was not strictly biological: according to one inscription written in the name of Nabonidus, "I am the real executor of the wills of Nebuchadnezzar and Neriglissar [= son-in-law and royal successor of Nebuchadnezzar], my royal predecessors."[8] Also, from the perspective of Daniel 5, Belshazzar is son of Nebuchadnezzar in the sense that he continues Nebuchadnezzar's obtuseness, his lack of spiritual insight—nay, rather, Belshazzar surpasses Nebuchadnezzar in his inability to understand God.

The Problem

Belshazzar was throwing a party. He got drunk, and as I've learned from Otis on *The Andy Griffith Show*, you sometimes do

---

Nabonidus married a daughter of Nebuchadnezzar so that Nebuchadnezzar would be the maternal grandfather of Belshazzar, but there's no evidence for this idea, so it is a complete guess. See, e.g., S. R. Driver, *The Book of Daniel* (Cambridge: Cambridge University Press, 1900), 62. Based on the early career of Nabonidus (a low-level courtier; Beaulieu, *Reign of Nabonidus*, 67–86), it seems unlikely that he would have married a princess.

7. See a similar example involving Jehu and Omri mentioned by Wendy L. Widder, *Daniel*, Story of God Bible Commentary (Grand Rapids: Zondervan, 2016), 108. See also the comment of Stephanie Dalley on the use of the term "son" in the early history of Babylon: "the word 'son' itself could be honorific, expressing a close relationship that need not be genetic"; *The City of Babylon: A History, c. 2000 BC – AD 116* (Cambridge: Cambridge University Press, 2021), 51–52.

8. The Babylon (or Istanbul) Stela, column 5, translated in ANET 309, and see the discussion in Beaulieu, *Reign of Nabonidus*, 111. The claim of legitimacy by a usurper was not rare; for a parallel, note Darius the Great of Persia and his claim of shared descent with Cyrus the Great; compare the Behistun Inscription (translation available at Wikisource) with the Cyrus Cylinder (translation available at Livius.org)—which present genealogies converging at the ancestor Teispes; see Matt Waters, *Ancient Persia: A Concise History of the Achaemenid Empire, 550–330 BCE* (Cambridge: Cambridge University Press, 2014), 8.

silly things when you're drunk. Belshazzar did a blasphemous thing. He had no doubt toured the royal treasuries and seen all the objects confiscated from foreign palaces and temples. Included in those royal treasuries were the objects from the Jewish temple in Jerusalem, as we already learned in the book of Daniel. This is how the book begins.

> In the third year of the reign of King Jehoiakim of Judah, King Nebuchadnezzar of Babylon came to Jerusalem and besieged it. [2]The Lord let King Jehoiakim of Judah fall into his power, as well as some of the vessels of the house of God. These he brought to the land of Shinar, and placed the vessels in the treasury of his gods (Dan 1:1–2).

Belshazzar had probably thought before as he saw these treasures: "It'd be neat to use those sometimes," just like all of us, when we tour a museum, want to touch all the objects under glass or wear the crown jewels. Of course, Belshazzar wouldn't ever do such a thing because it would be insulting to the gods. (Remember in 1 Samuel 5, when the Philistines captured the ark of the covenant, they put it in their own temple; they didn't mistreat it. Ancient people had a sense of decorum enough not to abuse the sacred objects of other peoples.)[9] When Belshazzar was drunk, he had no sense of decorum, and he cared nothing about the sacred.

The Result

A hand mysteriously appeared and wrote on the wall a message no one could understand. As we can well imagine, this incident scared Belshazzar silly (5:6). He was already silly, so maybe we

---

9. For an example, see Herodotus, *Histories* 7.197, who mentions Xerxes' decision not to violate a Greek temple. In Jewish tradition, see the story of the repulsion of Heliodorus from the Jewish temple at 2 Maccabees 3.

should say it seriously scared him. He announced a reward for anyone who could read the message (5:7). No one could (5:8). Once again we see the incompetence of the Babylonian wise men.

The queen entered (5:10). This is probably Belshazzar's mother or grandmother, as Josephus suggested.[10] His wives and concubines were already at the party (5:3). The queen knows about the history of Babylon, that Belshazzar's father Nebuchadnezzar employed a chief wise man who could interpret such mysteries (5:11–12). It seems that Belshazzar does not know who Daniel is. We might reflect on how quickly the world forgets. Probably few of us can name all the American presidents from the twentieth century. Most of us would have a hard time naming the preachers in our own congregation over the past fifty years. Serving in order to be remembered is foolish; people will forget. Reminds me of Ozymandias.

Daniel comes and is asked to interpret the mysterious writing (5:13–16). He took the opportunity to preach a sermon (5:17–23). In the previous chapter, when the king had been Nebuchadnezzar and Daniel had some bad news to report, Daniel was sorry, even scared (4:19). But here, before Belshazzar, Daniel seems to feel no fear; he's not at all sorry to tell Belshazzar that judgment is coming. Instead, he upbraids Belshazzar for being a fool. Perhaps Daniel thought that at least Nebuchadnezzar had tried, even if he was a little hard-headed, but Daniel had had enough of Belshazzar's shenanigans. Belshazzar had been given the advantage of knowing what happened in the case of Nebuchadnezzar, and he had taken no warning. Daniel reminds Belshazzar of Nebuchadnezzar's humiliation, which led to Nebuchadnezzar's transformation (5:20–21). Belshazzar should have learned a lesson, but no. Rather than humbling himself in the manner of Nebuchadnezzar, Belshazzar "exalted yourself against the Lord of heaven" (5:23).

---

10. Josephus, *Antiquities of the Jews* 10.237.

The Writing

The mystery of the writing was not so much what the words were but what they meant. It was written in Aramaic, like all of this section of the book of Daniel, and Aramaic was the administrative language of the empire. The Aramaic words that appeared on the wall were the names of three weights, but why a hand should appear and write the names of weights on the wall was certainly a mystery. The words may also have been written in a strange way, perhaps up and down rather than across. (They're written up and down in Rembrandt's painting of the scene, *Belshazzar's Feast*, c. 1635.)

Daniel explains the words:

- *mene*, written twice, like the Hebrew measurement *mina*, as in the Parable of the Minas (or Pounds, Luke 19:11–27).
- *tekel*, like Hebrew shekel.
- *upharsin*. The 'u' at the beginning is "and," so this is "and *pharsin*." *Pharsin* could be a measurement, a "half-mina," or it could be a word meaning "division."

So the trick is knowing what is the deeper significance of these terms for measurement. Samuel Driver explains:

The puzzle consisted partly in the character or manner in which they were supposed to have been written—an unfamiliar form of the Aramaic character, for instance, or, as the mediæval Jews suggested, a vertical instead of a horizontal arrangement of the letters; partly in the difficulty of attaching any meaning to them, even when they were read: what could the names of three weights signify?[11] Here Daniel's skill in the 'declaring of riddles' (v. 12) comes in. *Měnê* itself means 'numbered,' as well as 'a m'na':

---

11. Driver (*Book of Daniel*, 69 n. 2) points to parallels in which the names of

it is accordingly interpreted as signifying that the days of Belshazzar's kingdom are 'numbered,' and approaching their end.
Tĕkēl, '*shekel*,' suggests *tĕkîl*, 'weighed': 'Thou art *weighed* in the
balances, and art found wanting.' *Parsin*, 'half-m'nas,' or *pĕrês*
(*pĕrâs*), 'a half-m'na,' points allusively to a double interpretation:
'Thy kingdom is *divided* (*pĕrîs*), and given to the Medes and
Persians' (Aramaic *pāras*).[12]

Daniel delivers the interpretation, guaranteeing not only
imminent death to Belshazzar but also a complete end of the
kingdom. Belshazzar is thankful to Daniel and gives him the
reward (5:29) that he had promised (5:7, 16) which Daniel had
already tried to refuse (5:17). That seems strange since Daniel
had just delivered terrible news. Jerome suggested that Belshazzar assumed the fulfillment would come after a long time, or
that he could mitigate the punishment by honoring this
prophet.[13] As Jerome also suggested, the fact that Daniel was
honored so extravagantly immediately before the transfer of the
kingdom to the Medes and Persians means that Daniel was well-
placed to be noticed by the new government.

The Fulfillment

It all happened fast. That very night, Belshazzar died and the
kingdom was "received" by someone named Darius the Mede.
Belshazzar paid for his brazen action very quickly and decisively.

The Lesson

God sees everything. There is no hiding from Him. Jesus called

---

common objects were interpreted significantly: Jeremiah 1:11–12; 19:1, 7; Amos
8:1.

12. Driver, *Book of Daniel*, 69.

13. Jerome, *Commentary on Daniel*, trans. Gleason L. Archer (Grand Rapids:
Baker, 1958), 61. See also Josephus' comment at *Antiquities of the Jews* 10.246.

Him, "Your Father who sees in secret" (Matt 6:4, 6, 18)—He sees the good and He sees the bad. Belshazzar may have been under the impression that his own Babylonian gods wouldn't really care about his behavior as long as he paid them proper respect in the form of sacrifices and festivals and such. And he probably thought that the defeated God of the Judeans would have nothing to say about what happened in another land (not Judah). He should have learned from Nebuchadnezzar's experience (as Daniel told him) that the God of the Judeans is concerned about the whole earth; there are no borders for Him.

God will execute punishment on the wicked. Oftentimes it feels like any judgment from God is far away; He is patient. Remember what Peter said?

> But do not ignore this one fact, beloved, that with the Lord one day is like a thousand years, and a thousand years are like one day. The Lord is not slow about his promise, as some think of slowness, but is patient with you, not wanting any to perish, but all to come to repentance (2 Pet 3:8–9).

Peter had already pointed out that some people think that because God has not yet brought judgment, that He will never do it (2 Pet 3:3–4). The fact is, we don't know when judgment is coming, any more than Belshazzar did. His experience is a warning to us, that we should remain vigilant, ready, prepared.

> For you yourselves know very well that the day of the Lord will come like a thief in the night. When they say, "There is peace and security," then sudden destruction will come upon them, as labor pains come upon a pregnant woman, and there will be no escape! But you, beloved, are not in darkness, for that day to surprise you like a thief; for you are all children of light and children of the day; we are not of the night or of darkness. So then let us not fall asleep as others do, but let us keep awake and be

sober; for those who sleep sleep at night, and those who are
drunk get drunk at night (1 Thess 5:2–7).

Belshazzar was drunk at night, not at all expecting his life to
come to an end. He should have taken warning from Nebuchadnezzar, and we should take warning from Belshazzar. Things can
change quickly.

Discussion Questions

- Why does Belshazzar want to drink wine from the
  temple vessels (Dan 5:1–4)?
- Why do you think Belshazzar needs to be told about
  Daniel by the queen (5:10–12)?
- What does Daniel tell Belshazzar (5:17–23)? Why does
  he remind Belshazzar about the time Nebuchadnezzar
  lived in the field?
- What is the writing on the wall, and what does it
  mean?
- Why do you think God seems so impatient with
  Belshazzar whereas He had been so patient with
  Nebuchadnezzar?

Chapter 6
In the Lion's Den

So the presidents and the satraps tried to find grounds for complaint against Daniel in connection with the kingdom. But they could find no grounds for complaint or any corruption, because he was faithful, and no negligence or corruption could be found in him (Dan 6:4).

W hat will you do when push comes to shove, when you've got to make a decision, when you're either in or out, no more fence-sitting? The Bible presents such a choice pretty frequently ... because people like to sit on the fence. We like to hedge our bets. We like to be lukewarm, neither hot nor cold. But Jesus hates it (Rev 3:16). God wants us to pick a side. "Choose you this day whom you will serve" (Josh 24:15). Elijah asks the Israelites, "How long will you go limping with two different opinions?" (1 Kgs 18:21). We want to serve two masters, but Jesus says we can't (Matt 6:24). Jesus says there are two paths, two ways on which to travel (Matt 7:13–14), and what He really wants to know is, "Are you gonna go my way?"

Daniel 6 shows us a man who has spent a lifetime choosing to be faithful to his God. When the decree came down forcing him to choose sides, he didn't flinch. He maintained his faithfulness, forged through many years of religious habits. Though disobeying the new law meant certain death, Daniel accepted his fate and defied the king. In the face of adversity, he did the boldest thing he could: he got down on his knees and prayed.

Daniel is now an old man.[1] Nebuchadnezzar's Babylonian Empire has now passed away, and still Daniel survives. He had been taken into captivity with his friends at a young age, he had faced many challenges, but he had always maintained his faith in God and had served faithfully in his new-found home. Early in the exile, the prophet Jeremiah had sent a letter to the exiled Jews in Babylon (Jer 29:1), and we might imagine that Daniel was one of the privileged recipients of this letter; at least, in Daniel 9:2, our hero was reading "in the books ... the word of YHWH to the prophet Jeremiah." At any rate, Daniel had certainly lived out Jeremiah's council to "seek the welfare of the city where I have sent you into exile, and pray to YHWH on its behalf, for in its welfare you will find your welfare" (Jer 29:7). Daniel had lived a good, prosperous life, mostly comfortable (we might imagine) despite the few occasions in which his life had been threatened (e.g., Dan 2:12–16).[2] He had earned his position as a trusted adviser to Nebuchadnezzar (Dan 4:8–9), and he had also been honored by the later Babylonian king Belshazzar (Dan 5:29). Well past retirement age, he now serves a new king in a new empire. He had been in the (metaphorical) lion's den nearly all his life, and now he finds himself there more than ever.

---

1. This statement is based on the storyline in the book of Daniel. The book (Dan 9:2) cites Jeremiah's prophecy that the exile would last seventy years (cf. Jer 25:11; 29:10), and since Daniel lived through this entire period, we must think of Daniel as an old man in ch. 6, something like 85–90 years old.

2. Aside from the story about the lion's den (Daniel 6), the only time Daniel had found his life threatened in the book was in Daniel 2, before he had become well-known as a wise man. Presumably his life was threatened also in Daniel 3, but he is unmentioned in that chapter, which focuses instead on Shadrach, Meshach, and Abednego.

The King

The king in this chapter is someone named Darius the Mede, who had become king at the end of the previous chapter after the death of Belshazzar (5:30–31). As Daniel had predicted, Belshazzar's kingdom had been handed over to the Medes and Persians (5:28), and Darius is the king of this new kingdom. But Darius the Mede is unknown outside of the book of Daniel. The book of Daniel also mentions a king named Cyrus the Persian (6:28; 10:1), and other sources inform us that it was Cyrus who defeated Babylon and who released the Jews from their captivity (cf. Ezra 1:1–4). Different theories have sought to account for the appearance of this (otherwise unknown) king, Darius the Mede. Some ancient interpreters suggested that he was known in Greek sources and ancient Near Eastern sources under some other name.[3] Daniel himself had two names (1:7), so there is some precedent for the idea that Darius might have two names, but it's just a guess. At any rate, the exact identity of Darius the Mede is largely irrelevant to understanding and benefiting from this story in which he is one of the main characters.

The Plot

In the new regime, Daniel quickly stood out, again. Remember, as Belshazzar's final act as king (5:29), he had appointed Daniel to a high position in the Babylonian court, over a third of the kingdom (or in third position in the kingdom; translations differ). When the rule passed from the Babylonians to the Medes and Persians, Daniel was one of the three chiefs under the new king Darius, and soon he would be not just one of three but the highest official under the king (6:1–3). The other officials started their plot against him.

---

3. See Josephus, *Antiquities of the Jews* 10.248; Jerome, *Commentary on Daniel*, trans. Gleason Archer (Grand Rapids: Baker, 1958), 55.

The text does not precisely say why the other officials had it in for Daniel, but it's not hard to guess. Pretty obviously they were jealous of Daniel's prestige, and maybe even of his competence. Reportedly, they started chanting, "Oh no, what we gonna do? The king likes Daniel more than me and you!" The Septuagint (the Greek translation) specifies that the leaders of the opposition against Daniel were the other two chiefs in the triumvirate under Darius (6:3). When Darius decided to appoint Daniel as their boss, they got jealous. It may also be that racism played a part, or something more like ethnocentrism. After all, these men describe Daniel to the king—as if the king didn't know who Daniel was!—as "one of the exiles from Judah" (6:13). Do they say these words with a sneer? After decades away from Judah, Daniel is still considered by these men as "one of the exiles from Judah." They do not appreciate this foreigner coming in and taking their job.

And they also might be spiteful, because they don't like the fact that Daniel is a goody-two-shoes. As Christopher Wright puts it:

> We live in a world which is in rebellion against God. So it will show all the marks of that rebellion when faced with anyone who stands for the values of God's kingdom—truth, honesty, integrity, goodness, and even plain competence. Such things are not welcome in our world.[4]

But mostly they're just jealous, envious of this man who so easily wins the favor of people in power. So they plot to destroy him. (This sounds familiar—Mark 3:6.) Their first plan was to figure out some way to accuse Daniel of being a bad government employee, but they couldn't come up with anything (Dan 6:4). Time for Plan B: they knew how committed Daniel was to his

---

4. Christopher J. H. Wright, *Hearing the Message of Daniel: Sustaining Faith in Today's World* (Downers Grove, IL: IVP, 2017), 133.

religion, so they figured out a way to get his religion to conflict with his job.

They convinced King Darius that all the other officials agreed that for a solid month, no one in the kingdom should pray to anyone other than Darius (6:6–8). Darius signed the bill into law (6:9).

What was Darius thinking? Why would he make such an idiotic law? As you read through the entire chapter, it looks like Darius is a pretty good guy, rooting for Daniel. He didn't intend to put Daniel in a difficult situation (6:14). It seems he didn't think through the implications of this new law. The problem was that this new law was very flattering toward Darius. It was a great honor, especially because other people had thought it up and not Darius himself. The approach of these officials to Darius reminds me of a used car salesman, effusive with his compliments about how smart you are and how great you look behind the wheel of this car. Darius fell for it.

Daniel's Response

Daniel learns about the new law and changes nothing about his routine. He goes into his room and prays toward Jerusalem three times a day (6:10). Why does he look toward Jerusalem? There is no law that mandates this position, but perhaps Daniel was reflecting on what Solomon had prayed at the dedication of the temple. At the end of his long prayer in 1 Kings 8, Solomon acknowledged that there would probably come a time when God exiled the people of Israel away from their land due to their sin (8:46–53). Solomon asked that in that situation—the very situation in which Daniel now finds himself—if the people repent and turn toward the temple and the city for prayer, that God will hear them and restore them to their homeland. Of course, when Daniel offered his prayers in Daniel 6, there was no temple in

Jerusalem, since it had been destroyed by Nebuchadnezzar. But Daniel prayed toward the city where the temple had been.[5]

What do you think he was praying about? I imagine his prayers at this particular time have a little added urgency. The text explicitly says that he had heard about the ordinance banning such prayers. No doubt this situation entered into Daniel's prayers; surely he was, in part, praying for God's protection. Perhaps also Daniel was doing what the apostle Paul would later encourage Christians to do, to pray for their political leaders (1 Tim 2:1–2). Daniel was probably praying for Darius. And maybe Daniel was also doing what Jesus told his audience to do (Matt 5:44), and what Jesus himself did (Luke 23:34). Maybe Daniel was praying for his enemies.

The text says that this is something Daniel had already been in the habit of doing, praying three times a day (6:10). He didn't start praying only when he found himself in a dire circumstance. In fact, he wouldn't even be in this dire circumstance if he weren't a man deeply committed to prayer. One of the lessons of this chapter is that prayer is essential to the life of faith and committed, routine prayer is essential—not simply spontaneous, when-I-feel-like-it prayer. Daniel prayed three times a day whether he faced a tough situation or not.

I appreciate Pete Greig's advice on prayer: "Keep it simple. Keep it real. Keep it up."[6] I guess the Bible doesn't really tell us whether Daniel kept his prayers simple and real, but it certainly tells us that he kept it up. Did Daniel always enjoy praying? Did he always know exactly what to say? Well, he was a person, like us, so ... probably not. Here's Greig again:

> There are definitely days I'd prefer a set of personal super-

---

5. Jerome already suggested this connection between Daniel's prayer posture and Solomon's prayer at the temple dedication; see Jerome, *Commentary on Daniel*, trans. Archer, 65–66.

6. Pete Greig, *How to Pray: A Simple Guide for Normal People* (Carol Stream, IL: NavPress, 2019). All of the quotations are from Chapter Two.

powers to slogging away at the slow, confusing business of prayer. God knows that we don't always find it easy to string a sentence together in his presence. "He remembers," as the psalmist says, "that we are dust" (Ps 103:14). He understands that we sometimes get tongue-tied, distracted, overwhelmed, and confused. He doesn't get insecure if we occasionally doubt his existence. He sees our bruised and broken hearts and accepts that prayer hasn't always seemed to help. He isn't in the least bit annoyed that we occasionally find talking to him a bit boring. Or that we would sometimes prefer to scale the Empire State Building covered in spandex than merely, meekly to "go into [our] room, close the door and pray to [our] Father, who is unseen" [Matt 6:6].

But the thing is this: *He likes us*. A lot.

And if I may quote Greig once more—

I don't want to put anything heavy or unsustainable on you as you seek to grow in prayer. But here is the great and inescapable truth—taught in Scripture, modeled by Christ, and advocated without exception by all the heroes of our faith: You cannot grow in prayer without some measure of effort and discomfort, self-discipline and self-denial.

The story in Daniel 6 certainly encourages its readers to be like Daniel, and that means being committed to prayer.

Saving Daniel

We all know what happens next: Daniel is thrown into the lion's den and suffers no harm. The next morning Daniel reports to the king: "My God sent his angel and shut the lions' mouths so that they would not hurt me" (6:22). Even the king suspected, or hoped, that the situation would turn out this way: when executing the punishment the day before, the king had exclaimed, "Your God ... will deliver you," or—perhaps it should be translated—"May your God deliver you" (6:16).[7] That's a far cry from Nebuchadnezzar's boast, "What god is able to deliver you out of my hands?!" (3:15). In chapter 6, Darius actually issues a decree at the end of the story requiring his entire kingdom to acknowledge the God of Daniel as the living God who is sovereign.

Daniel went down into the pit, but he came up again. The word for the "den" of lions (6:7, 12, etc.)—at least in the LXX—is often translated "pit," as in the story about Joseph being thrown into a pit by his jealous brothers (Gen 37:20).[8] Sometimes this same word, "pit," is used as a synonym for Sheol (or Hades), the place of the dead.

> YHWH, you have brought up my soul from Sheol;
> > you restored me to life from among those who go down to the pit (Ps 30:3).

> He drew me up from the pit of destruction,
> > out of the miry bog,
> > and set my feet upon a rock,
> > making my steps secure (Ps 40:2).

> Answer me quickly, YHWH!
> > My spirit fails!
> > Hide not your face from me,
> > lest I be like those who go down to the pit (Ps 143:7).

Daniel was certainly a dead man being thrown into the pit of lions, but miraculously God brought up his life from the pit.

---

7. Both translations are possible, but the first one is traditional, represented in ancient translations (Septuagint, Latin Vulgate) and the KJV.
8. Here I am referring to the Greek word in the Septuagint (λάκκος, *lakkos*). The oldest form of Daniel 6 is Aramaic, and since so little Aramaic appears in the Bible, it doesn't do much good to search for the Aramaic word.

That sounds familiar. Remember what Peter said on the day of Pentecost?

> But God raised him up, having freed him from death, because it was impossible for him to be held in its power. For David says concerning him,

(And then Peter quotes Psalm 16...)

> I saw the Lord always before me,
>   for he is at my right hand so that I will not be
> shaken;
>   therefore my heart was glad, and my tongue rejoiced;
>   moreover my flesh will live in hope.
>   For you will not abandon my soul to Hades,
>   or let your Holy One experience corruption.
>   You have made known to me the ways of life;
>   you will make me full of gladness with your
> presence (Acts 2:24–28; cf. Ps 16:8–11).

God did not abandon the soul of Jesus to Hades, and neither did He abandon Daniel to the pit. In this way, Daniel becomes a type of Christ, and his deliverance from the pit of lions becomes a type of the Resurrection.

This similarity helps us to see more similarities. Daniel was condemned to death by a government bureaucrat (King Darius), even though the bureaucrat knew he was innocent. The king knew that Daniel's accusers were motivated by jealousy (cf. Mark 15:10). Before being sentenced to death, Daniel prayed alone three times, perhaps asking that God let this cup pass from him. Daniel's prayers take place not in a garden but in an upper room. When Daniel is finally cast into the pit, a boulder closed over the pit, and the entrance was sealed (Dan 6:17; cf. Matt 27:62–66).

When Daniel emerges from the pit unscathed, delivered

from death by his God, he might have proclaimed the words of Hosea:

> O Death, where are your plagues?
>   O Sheol, where is your destruction?
>   (Hos 13:14; cf. 1 Cor 15:55).

Daniel 6 presents to us a picture of our Lord, and just like Jesus, Daniel had to endure death (or close to it) before he could experience the victory over death. We remember that Jesus told His followers that they would have to take up their cross and follow Him (Mark 8:34). Following Jesus sometimes means making the tough decision to suffer for your commitment to God. Peter puts the matter this way: "For to this you have been called, because Christ also suffered for you, leaving you an example, so that you should follow in his steps" (1 Pet 2:21).

Peter repeatedly mentions the possibility that his readers might suffer even though they have done nothing wrong. In this way, they can also imitate Jesus (2:15; 4:16, 19).

> Now who will harm you if you are eager to do what is good? But even if you do suffer for doing what is right, you are blessed. Do not fear what they fear, and do not be intimidated, but in your hearts sanctify Christ as Lord. Always be ready to make your defense to anyone who demands from you an accounting for the hope that is in you; yet do it with gentleness and reverence. Keep your conscience clear, so that, when you are maligned, those who abuse you for your good conduct in Christ may be put to shame. For it is better to suffer for doing good, if suffering should be God's will, than to suffer for doing evil (1 Pet 3:13–17).

In Daniel 6 there is also the unpleasant business of judgment upon the wicked (6:24). This is a chapter that reminds us of many aspects of the Christian religion: commitment to prayer,

suffering for doing right, judgment upon the wicked, and resurrection. God will set things right. Daniel 6 reminds us how.

* * *

Be merciful to me, O God, be merciful to me,
> for in you my soul takes refuge;
> > in the shadow of your wings I will take refuge,
> > > until the destroying storms pass by.
> I cry to God Most High,
> > to God who fulfills his purpose for me.
> He will send from heaven and save me,
> > he will put to shame those who trample on
me. *Selah*
> God will send forth his steadfast love and his faith-
fulness.
> I lie down among lions
> > that greedily devour human prey;
> > their teeth are spears and arrows,
> > > their tongues sharp swords.
> Be exalted, O God, above the heavens.
> > Let your glory be over all the earth.
> They set a net for my steps;
> > my soul was bowed down.
> > They dug a pit in my path,
> > > but they have fallen into it themselves. *Selah*
> My heart is steadfast, O God,
> > my heart is steadfast.
> I will sing and make melody.
> Awake, my soul!
> > Awake, O harp and lyre!
> > I will awake the dawn.
> I will give thanks to you, O Lord, among the peoples;
> > I will sing praises to you among the nations.
> For your steadfast love is as high as the heavens;

your faithfulness extends to the clouds.
Be exalted, O God, above the heavens.
Let your glory be over all the earth (Ps 57).

Discussion Questions

- Why did the presidents and satraps want to get Daniel in trouble in Daniel 6? What did they have against Daniel?
- How did they convince Darius to pass this new law?
- From this chapter as a whole, how would you characterize Darius? What kind of king is he? What kind of person is he?
- Why do you think Daniel prayed toward Jerusalem (Dan 6:10)? See 1 Kings 8:46–53.
- What sort of proclamation did Darius issue after God saved Daniel from the lions?

Chapter 7
The Four Beasts and the Son of Man

R ed pill or blue pill? If you want the blue pill, you better stop reading Daniel here. Of course, the entire book—the entire Bible, really—is a very red-pill kind of text, but that is especially true of apocalyptic literature. We are leaving behind the Sunday school stories, and things are about to get weird(er). Daniel 7 is the first of four apocalyptic visions. I'll tell you more about what "apocalyptic" means in just a moment, but the most important thing to know is that it has to do with revelation: apocalyptic literature reveals, unveils, the truth about something. It pulls back the curtain and discloses what's really going on. And that's why you should stop reading here if you want the blue pill. Daniel's about to shove the red pill down our throats.

Not everybody wants to know the truth. Even in *The Matrix*, Cypher eventually decided that his life would have been better had he chosen the blue pill. He longed for the fake world created by the computers as opposed to the harsh truth of reality. Remember that scene where he's having a meal with Agent Smith, and he lifts up the bit of steak on his fork, and he says something like, "I know this steak is simply a projection of my mind, but I don't care"? There are people like that, which should not surprise us. There's a reason for the proverb, "Ignorance is bliss."

The problem for Christians is, God doesn't want us ignorant. He wants us to know something about the world we're living in, and Daniel's going to show us.

Apocalyptic Literature

The Introduction mentions a few points about apocalyptic literature that I'll repeat here. I just mentioned above that the most important thing about apocalyptic is its connection to revelation. That's how it gets its name. Apocalypse is a Greek word that means "revelation." The Book of Revelation is also known as the Apocalypse, and the word *apocalypse* (ἀποκάλυψις) is the very first word of the book in Greek. (It was, in fact, the book of Revelation that gave the genre of apocalyptic literature its name.) So thinking about the distinctive features of the book of Revelation will help us think about apocalyptic literature in general. Probably the first thing you think of for the book of Revelation is the strange imagery. We're going to get that in spades in the back half of Daniel. The appearance of angels is characteristic of apocalypses. That's different from classical prophecy. Isaiah and Jeremiah and Hosea all received messages from God without any mention of an angel. We'll see, though, that Daniel does not hear directly from God but a heavenly intermediary is sent to him to explain things. Another difference from classical prophecy is that the prophets often (not always) aimed at getting God's people to repent of sin, but in apocalyptic (certainly in Daniel and Revelation) there is little of that. The message instead is about hope. (Of course, the classical prophets also offered hope.) The idea is that although things look bad for us, actually, if you could see what's going on in heaven, you'd realize that victory is ours.

And so we come back to revelation. Apocalypses reveal to us what is going on behind the scenes, out of normal sight. We might think that the kingdoms of the world are all-powerful, but Daniel learns that they aren't. The kingdoms of the world might present themselves as wonderful benefits to humankind, but Daniel learns that they aren't. We might think that the current domination by the kingdoms of the earth means that the God of Israel isn't really in control, but Daniel learns that's not true. All of this resonates with the book of Revelation. Probably no book of the Old Testament has had such a strong impact on the book of Revelation as has the book of Daniel. We're going to see some of those connections as we read Daniel 7.

Daniel's Second Half

The second half of the book of Daniel is all apocalyptic visions, more-or-less (ch. 9 is a bit different). All these chapters (even ch. 9) have angels revealing heavenly mysteries to Daniel about the future. There's a lot of strange imagery. There are four visions in these six chapters since the last vision extends over the final three chapters of the book. The visions are dated, thus:

- ch. 7: Belshazzar, year 1
- ch. 8: Belshazzar, year 3
- ch. 9: Darius, year 1
- chs. 10–12: Cyrus, year 3

The apocalyptic visions do not, then, continue the chronology of the first half of the book, but go back to earlier times. Chapters 7–8 are dated before Chapter 5, for instance. Nevertheless, the time when these visions were delivered to Daniel is almost irrelevant since all of the content of these visions points to a time beyond Daniel's lifetime.

The Vision

Basically, Daniel dreams about four strange creatures and then a judgment scene.

The Beasts

The four strange creatures each come up from the sea (7:2). They are described thus (7:4–8):

1. lion with eagles' wings, but the wings were plucked, it stood up straight and was given a human mind.
2. bear, raised up on one side, three ribs in its mouth.
3. leopard, four wings, four heads.
4. fourth beast, iron teeth, (claws of bronze, 7:19,) ten horns, then a little horn that displaced three other horns, and the little horn had eyes and a mouth. The little horn "made war with the holy ones and was prevailing over them, until the Ancient of Days came" (7:21–22, interpreted at 7:23–27). Note especially that the little horn "shall attempt to change the sacred seasons and the law, and they shall be given into his power for a time, two times, and half a time" (7:25; cf. 12:7).

None of these beasts look exactly like animals with which we are familiar, certainly not Beast #4. Even the first three are described as "like a lion" and "like a bear" and "like a leopard." A lion with wings like an eagle is not any kind of lion with which we are familiar. Same for a leopard with four heads and four wings. Apparently Beast #2, the one like a bear, looks more like an animal familiar to us, or at least it's not described as looking very strange; but neither is it described in much detail.

I do not know what all this imagery means. I have a feeling that some of it doesn't *mean* anything, that its purpose is not to point to some reality but just to exist within Daniel's dream. I think some of the imagery might be intended to disorient the reader, to signal that we're not in the world that we know, but we're in some strange new reality. So, maybe the three ribs or tusks in the mouth of the bear (7:5) mean something, but I don't know what they mean, and I'm not convinced that they mean anything, except that this bear has started eating. The ribs in the bear's mouth signal that this bear is dangerous, as also does the command to the bear to "devour much flesh." Why three? Why not three?

Likewise, why are the first three animals described as similar to a lion, a bear, and a leopard? Are we supposed to understand anything in particular about these specific animals? I doubt it. I think the meaning is that we've got three different animals, and they're all scary, all animals that you shouldn't mess with because all of them are the kinds of animals that might eat you. No kittens or turtles here.

The fourth beast might also eat you, and it apparently is not like any animal that we know, so it is all the more strange and ferocious. It also has this strange little horn—a horn with eyes and a mouth. It's this little horn that becomes the focus later in the vision, but for now, there is only the mention that the horn uses its mouth to boast.

The Judgment Scene

The second half of the vision (before the interpretation) shifts the perspective away from these strange animals to a judgment scene (7:9–14). Thrones were set up, and then the Ancient of Days (עַתִּיק יוֹמִין) came, whose own throne was fire. Books were opened (7:10). During this time, that little horn on the fourth beast kept talking (7:11), but then the animal was killed, which silenced that horn. The other beasts continued to live but without so much power. Finally, into the power vacuum created by the removal of these beasts came one not like an animal but like a person, like a human being, like a son of man (7:13). This one like a human received everlasting dominion (7:14).

Interpreting the Vision

At this point, Daniel—in his dream—approached one of the heavenly host (7:16), apparently one of the "thousand thousands" that "served him" (7:10), to whom we had been introduced earlier. This angel explained the meaning of everything, and here's what it all means: "As for these four great beasts, four kings shall arise out of the earth. But the holy ones of the Most High shall receive the kingdom and possess the kingdom forever —forever and ever" (7:17–18; cf. 7:22).

It's interesting, isn't it, how brief this interpretation is compared to how detailed the dream itself is. I take that as some justification for my earlier hesitation to ascribe meaning to every detail of the dream.

The interpretation makes it clear that this dream is very similar to Nebuchadnezzar's dream in Daniel 2. The basic idea is that the kingdom of God is established and entails the diminishment of earthly kingdoms. Or, to look at it from the opposite end:

> The basic issue with which this chapter is concerned, as with the dream in ch. 2, is God's decision to delegate universal sovereignty to Gentile empires for a period of time and then to take back that sovereignty.[1]

Here, beasts = kingdoms (or kings). The beasts are all terrifying in their own way, and they all are focused on consumption. These beasts are not interested in creating peaceful societies, or in bettering people's lives or promoting human flourishing, or in

---

1. Carol A. Newsom and Brennan W. Breed, *Daniel*, Old Testament Library (Louisville: WJK, 2014), 219.

encouraging attention to important matters divine. They are interested in eating.

I said earlier that Daniel, and especially this chapter, had an influence on the book of Revelation. In that book, we also meet a beast, one that has characteristics of a leopard, and a bear, and a lion (Rev 13:2). It's no coincidence that those specific animals are mentioned! Daniel 7 helps us to read Revelation 13, since we know that beasts = kingdoms. For Revelation, the kingdom is Rome.

In Daniel, there are four beasts, and there has been a lot of controversy over which specific kingdoms are intended (just like in Daniel 2). I would suggest, as I suggested in respect to Daniel 2, that it doesn't particularly matter. The characteristics of these kingdoms remain true for all kingdoms all over the world throughout time. This is the red pill of apocalyptic. Whatever earthly kingdom you're talking about, Daniel wants you to know that it's a beast concerned primarily with devouring. However powerful you think a kingdom is, Daniel wants you to know that its power is only temporarily granted by the God of heaven.

But isn't this a prediction about something that's going to happen in the future, some specific future incident (the establishment of God's kingdom) at a specific future time? Hmm, well, maybe, maybe not. Now, I don't deny that some things in the book of Daniel are written as specific future predictions, like in Daniel 8 and Daniel 11. But it seems to me that in the case of Daniel's dream, what we're supposed to understand is not a timetable for when God will establish His rule but that things look different from heaven's perspective. Human governments are monsters whose rule is temporary, and they stand under the judgment of God.

Are we supposed to think about four specific kingdoms? Again, my answer is maybe, maybe not. Let's think about how numbers are used in this vision. Probably in regard to the four winds that stir up the sea (7:2), the number of winds simply

denotes totality, not a specific number of winds.[2] In respect to
the four heads on the leopard (7:6), probably the number four
denotes totality, not a specific number.[3] With regard to the ten
horns on the fourth beast (7:7), which stands for kings (7:24),
probably the number ten denotes totality, not a specific
number.[4] So I think the four kingdoms might represent specific
kingdoms, but the number four might just indicate universality:
this is how all earthly kingdoms behave. What we need is not
another kingdom of this world, but a kingdom altogether
different.

From heaven's perspective, earthly kingdoms are always
temporary, and for the most part, they continue to exist even
after their power is removed (7:12)—that is, except for cases in
which God specially intervenes to take care of problems, like
that boastful little horn (7:11). Earthly kingdoms often produce
boastful little horns, and some examples that have been especially important in the interpretation of the book of Daniel have
been the second-century BC Greek ruler Antiochus IV
Epiphanes, the mid-first-century AD Roman ruler Nero, and the
late-first-century Roman ruler Domitian. (In our own day, there
is no shortage of boastful little horns. Maybe you can think of
some.) When such boastful little horns are removed from office,
Daniel encourages us to see the hand of God at work.

Let me defend my reticence to offer a specific interpretation
of this horn. In Daniel 8 we again meet a boastful little horn, and
it is clear that the horn in that case is Antiochus IV Epiphanes.
How is it clear? Because Daniel tells us there that the relevant
kingdom is that of the Greeks. The final vision of the book (in
ch. 11) is also certainly dealing with definite people in history,
people that can be identified because of the details provided in

2. Newsom and Breed, *Daniel*, 221.
3. Newsom and Breed, *Daniel*, 224.
4. Newsom and Breed, *Daniel*, 225. On the other hand, Newsom and Breed,
Daniel, 225, think the three horns displaced by the little horn (7:8) denote three
specific people (Seleucus IV and his two sons).

the vision. I find no such details in Daniel 7, and certainly, the character Daniel was not meant to understand any specific application of the vision to definite people that would come long after his time. It seems to me to be sensible and edifying—and in harmony with the understanding of the character Daniel in the text—to read Daniel 7 as concerning kingdoms in general and little horns in general. Like many poems, such as the psalms, that are also written in very generic language, this chapter gains power through its ability to describe a variety of situations.[5]

Despite the continuing presence of the beasts, Daniel's dream and its angelic interpretation makes clear that the beasts do not have ultimate authority. It is the Ancient of Days who determines times and seasons, who grants authority and takes it away.

The character Daniel is most interested in the strange Beast #4, the one that expires before the others (7:11–12). Daniel further describes this beast and its arrogant horn (7:19–22). He noticed that this boastful horn made war against the holy ones until God judged in favor of the holy ones (7:21–22). The angel adds further description (7:23–27), especially that this horn (= king, 7:24) will "wear out the holy ones of the Most High, and shall attempt to change the sacred seasons and the law; and they shall be given into his power for a time, two times, and half a time" (7:25), i.e., three and a half years. Again, I don't take the reference to three and a half years literally; I think it means a short period of time, certainly short in comparison to the eternal dominion of the one like a son of man.

A Human—Not Beastly—Kingdom

> Do not be afraid, little flock, for it is your Father's good pleasure to give you the kingdom (Luke 12:32).

---

5. For a nuanced discussion, see R. W. L. Moberly, *The Bible in a Disenchanted Age: The Enduring Possibility of Christian Faith* (Grand Rapids: Baker, 2018), 119–26.

Daniel dreams that a human-like being "was given dominion and glory and kingship" (7:13–14). This is the kingdom that corresponds to that rock cut without hands in Daniel 2, the rock that grew into a mountain, that represents the kingdom of God. This is the kingdom that will never be destroyed and thus is completely unlike the beastly kingdoms.

Who is this son of man?

Who is the one who receives the kingdom? Answers vary, even within this chapter. At first, it's this human-like one (7:13–14), and then it's the holy ones (7:18, 22, 27); first an individual, then a group. We need to talk more about this human-like one. He is, literally, "like a son of a man" (כְּבַר אֱנָשׁ ", kevar enash"), just as the beastly kingdoms are "like a lion" and "like a bear" and "like a leopard." The phrase "son of a man" or "son of man" simply means a human being. It's a common way that God addresses Ezekiel, for instance: "Son of man, stand on your feet" (Ezek 2:1). (The Hebrew expression is *ben adam*.) Phil Collins has a great song on the *Tarzan* (1999) soundtrack called "Son of Man," all about how Tarzan will start acting like a son of man rather than a son of a gorilla. Same meaning at Psalm 146:3: "Put not your trust in princes, nor in the son of man, in whom there is no help." Even Daniel is called "son of man" at Daniel 8:17.

Of course, when you hear someone described as "son of man," you're not thinking about Ezekiel or Tarzan, and you're certainly not thinking about someone "in whom there is no help." You're thinking about Jesus, and for good reason. He called himself "the Son of Man," a lot—about eighty times in the Gospels. Some examples:

> The Son of Man came not to be served but to serve ... (Mark 10:45).

When the Son of Man comes in his glory, and all the angels with him, then he will sit on the throne of his glory (Matt 25:31).

And I tell you, everyone who acknowledges me before others, the Son of Man also will acknowledge before the angels of God (Luke 12:8).

Very truly, I tell you, you will see heaven opened and the angels of God ascending and descending upon the Son of Man (John 1:51).

It's clear that Jesus is talking about Himself, but it's still a little strange; why would Jesus talk about Himself in the third person, and use this strange expression, "the Son of Man"—an expression that means, as we have seen, "the human"? In the Gospels, the expression almost exclusively appears on the lips of Jesus; no one ever calls Him that, not even the narrators of the Gospels.[6] People who heard Jesus thought it was strange for Him to call Himself that. At least once Jesus's audience got confused about who He was talking about. "Who is this son of man?" they asked (John 12:34).

Why did Jesus call Himself "the Son of Man"? No one particularly knows.[7] He certainly doesn't explain Himself. It seems apparent that people weren't expecting a figure called "the Son of Man"—in view of their confusion about the expression—as they were looking for a figure called the Christ or Messiah. No one ever said, "I wonder when the Son of Man will show up," the way they probably said, "I wonder when the Messiah will

---

6. The dying Stephen does use the expression at Acts 7:56. See also Rev 1:13; 14:14, but the expression isn't quite the same in Greek.

7. What will surely be the definitive work on this topic for some time to come is now in process of publication; see Richard Bauckham, *Son of Man*, vol. 1: *Early Jewish Literature* (Grand Rapids: Eerdmans, 2023). See also Larry W. Hurtado and Paul L. Owen, eds., *'Who Is This Son of Man?' The Latest Scholarship on a Puzzling Expression of the Historical Jesus* (London: Bloomsbury, 2011).

come."[8] So maybe Jesus wasn't using it as a title but as a description: He is identifying Himself as "the human one."

On the other hand, there is this very important passage:

> Again the high priest asked him, "Are you the Messiah, the Son of the Blessed One?" Jesus said, "I am; and you will see the Son of Man seated at the right hand of the Power, and coming with the clouds of heaven" (Mark 14:61–62).

It sure sounds like Jesus has Daniel 7:13–14 on his mind—a son of man coming with the clouds of heaven. With that passage in mind, why did Jesus call Himself the Son of Man? At least partly, it seems, He wanted to identify Himself with the figure in Daniel 7 who received eternal dominion. And after all, Jesus had come announcing the imminence of God's kingdom (Mark 1:15). If Jesus interpreted the son of man in Daniel 7 as a messianic figure, He wasn't the only one. At least some Rabbis also thought that the son of man in Daniel 7 was the Messiah.[9]

How would the original audience have understood this figure, this one like a son of man? Perhaps they would have understood it as a reference to the Messiah, and perhaps not. The expression, again, means merely "human-like." Perhaps they would have understood it as an angel?[10] Later in the book of Daniel, angels are described as looking like humans (e.g., 8:15), and we will meet angels that are apparently in charge of nations in some

---

8. But see *1 Enoch* 37–71, the so-called Parables (or Similitudes) of Enoch, written around the time of Jesus, and which has a figure called the Son of Man. Unfortunately, this document is preserved only in the Ethiopic language, which complicates comparison to Greek expressions. For a recent scholarly examination of the expression within the Parables of Enoch, see Bauckham, *Son of Man*, 5–131.

9. See the Babylonian Talmud, *Sanhedrin* 98a; *Numbers Rabbah* 13.14. See Alan F. Segal, *Two Powers in Heaven: Early Rabbinic Reports about Christianity and Gnosticism* (Leiden: Brill, 1977), 47–50, who associates this view with Rabbi Akiba (see also 48 n. 23 for Akiba's support of Bar Kokhba) and says that it was a minority view. For further discussion, see Bauckham, *Son of Man*, 314–27.

10. Newsom and Breed, *Daniel*, 219, take this view; see also Segal, *Two Powers*, 49 n. 25.

sense, as in the "Prince of Persia," for instance (10:13), and the "Prince of Greece" (10:20). Maybe the original audience would have suspected that the human-like one was an angel, the angelic guardian of God's people (Michael? 10:13)—and that notion might explain why both the human-like one receives dominion and the holy ones (saints? people of God?) receive dominion.[11] On the other hand, elsewhere in Daniel, "holy ones" are themselves angels (4:17).

However people may have understood the judgment scene in Daniel's dream, we can say at least a couple of things about this one like a son of man who receives dominion.

1. He is human-like, not beast-like. That is a major contrast, and it's on the surface of the text, not something you have to dig for. There is a fundamental difference between the beastly kingdoms and the kingdom of the human-like one. What characterizes the beastly kingdoms—devouring, consumption— should not characterize the eternal kingdom.

2. This human-like figure works in concert with, or even as a representative of, the holy ones of the Most High. That much is clear from what we've already seen: he receives the kingdom, they receive the kingdom. They work together, they are joined: he is the head, they are the body. And despite what "holy ones" means elsewhere in Daniel,[12] I think it must refer to humans here, to God's people.

3. Jesus considered Himself the ultimate fulfillment of

11. This is the interpretation pursued at the end of the first chapter of Peter Schäfer, *Two Gods in Heaven: Jewish Concepts of God in Antiquity* (Princeton: Princeton University Press, 2020), who points out that later in the book of Daniel the angels explicitly appear in human form (8:15; 9:21). See also Alan F. Segal, *Life after Death: A History of the Afterlife in Western Religion* (New York: Doubleday, 2004), 290.

12. And despite the argument of Newsom and Breed, *Daniel*, to the contrary; Newsom says that it means "angels" even here in Daniel 7, even in view of 7:25.

this vision. He would rule as king over a newly
established kingdom, and His followers, the holy
ones, would rule alongside Him (cf. Luke 22:28–30).

The beasts, representing earthly kingdoms, rule the world
in their horrible, beastly way. (Remember that in the New
Testament, it is Satan who has control of the earthly kingdoms
[Matt 4:8–9; John 12:31; etc.] whereas Jesus came to inaugurate a
"kingdom of heaven" [in Matthew's parlance, e.g., Matt 4:17].)
When God determines to do so, He removes the biggest
threat, Beast #4 with that boastful little horn, but He allows
the other beasts to remain alive with diminished authority.
Instead, He grants all authority over all peoples and for all time
to (a) one like a son of man (= human-like one, not beast-like)
and (b) the holy ones of the Most High, who had been perse-
cuted by the fourth beast but now enjoy dominion. Daniel's
dream shows heaven's perspective on the operations of the
world.

Lessons

If we decide to take the red pill Daniel is offering us, what does
it do to us? We will see who is really in charge of this world. We
will see the kingdoms of the earth the way heaven sees them, as
beasts concerned only with devouring and with only a temporary,
contingent dominion. And we will understand that God's holy
ones—despite what they may look like from earth's perspective
—will exercise an eternal dominion in concert with the one like
a son of man who rides on the clouds.

I have used concepts from *The Matrix* to help us think about
apocalyptic literature, but those same concepts are present in a
lot of works. We could think about the novel *1984*, how the
government tells their own story about the world, a story it
invents for the purpose of perpetuating its own authority. That's
beastlike. Or we could think about another George Orwell

novel, *Animal Farm*, that literally (or is it metaphorically?) focuses on beasts to make similar points.

How about *The Truman Show* (1998), about a man who lives in a fake world constructed for the very purpose of fooling him, so that he will continue in life without reflection. After all, as the mastermind behind this cruel experiment (= reality television show) intones at one point in the film: "We accept the reality of the world with which we're presented. It's as simple as that." Of course, this mastermind would be named Christof; he thinks of himself as Christ-like or even as a God. He created the world for his creature's enjoyment, and at the end of the movie, after his voice from the clouds appeals to the man to stay in the world created for him, he is crushed that the man rejects the fake world in favor of reality. As Paul wrote, "The god of this world has blinded the minds of the unbelievers, to keep them from seeing the light of the gospel of the glory of Christ, who is the image of God" (2 Cor 4:4).

Daniel's dream intends to help us choose reality instead of the fake world constructed so that we continue in life unreflectively. This dream pokes holes in the propaganda of Big Brother. It is the red pill that shakes us awake from the pleasant sleep induced by the matrix.

And what does the dream show us?

Earthly kingdoms are beastly in general, and some are worse. It is no great compliment that Winston Churchill bestowed on democracy when he called it the worst form of government except for all the others. His comment is an acknowledgment of the truth of Daniel 7—even the best form of human government is beastly, but there are worse forms of government. Americans routinely refer to their country as the greatest country in the world, and they routinely complain about their government. People generally acknowledge that Hitler's government was one of the worst forms, something like the fourth beast. Same for Stalin, and Pol Pot, and the Kims of North Korea, and those are just a few recent examples. Certainly, the government of Antiochus Epiphanes in the second century BC (at least, from a Jewish perspective) would fit this pattern, as would the governments of Nero and Domitian in the first century AD (from a Christian perspective).

The rule of the beastly kingdoms is temporary, however long it lasts. Sometimes it seems like it lasts a long time, but it's all a matter of perspective. See 2 Peter 3:8. One time I was walking down the road with my dog, and a bigger dog ran at us. I picked up my little dog, and the big dog jumped up and bit the back leg of my little dog, and hung on to the leg. The whole thing may have lasted a second and a half, but in the midst of it, it seemed like it was lasting much longer, as you can imagine. The rule of the beasts is like that. From earth's perspective, we imagine their rule as absolute and everlasting. From heaven's perspective, they're a blip on the radar.

This chapter—similar to Revelation—warns us about cozying up too much with human government. I do not mean to say that Christians shouldn't be involved in politics. I do mean to say that Christians need to have a proper perspective on what politics can accomplish, and always recognize that they have gotten involved with a beast. Daniel himself lived a political life, but as we've already seen, he kept Babylonian culture (and government) at arm's length. On a few occasions, at least, he was almost eaten by the beast. And now his dream reveals to him the true nature of the beast that he served.

God establishes a new dominion to rival—nay, rather, to replace—the dominions of the beasts. The one like a son of man is not like a beast at all. He doesn't even make war against the beasts (which might be considered a beastly approach to the beasts; cf. John 18:36). The beasts are rendered powerless before he shows up. His rule is altogether different, as it fulfills God's desires for the governance of the world and guarantees the security and happiness of God's people.

The point of it all: God will judge in favor of His saints.

Discussion Questions

- What is the main point of Daniel's dream in chapter 7, according to the angel who interprets the dream for Daniel?
- What is the meaning of the beasts in the dream? What do they symbolize? Why do you think God chooses to use beasts as a symbol?
- How would you describe the fourth beast? What are the most interesting characteristics of this fourth beast?
- What further information about the fourth beast does Daniel learn in the second half of the chapter?
- What is the fate of all these beasts?
- What information do we learn in Daniel 7 about the "one like a son of man"? What does he do?
- In Daniel 7, who receives eternal dominion? (There's more than one answer.)
- Search through the Bible for the phrase "son of man" to see where else it appears in the Old Testament. (You can use an online search tool for this.) Where does it appear most often? What does the phrase mean?
- We are probably most familiar with the phrase as Jesus's description of Himself. Why do you think Jesus uses the phrase "son of man" for Himself?
- One place Jesus uses the phrase "son of man" is in Mark 14:62. What is the situation in which Jesus finds Himself in this passage? What connections to Daniel 7 do you see in Jesus's words here? What reaction do the words of Jesus elicit?

Chapter 8
The Goat and the Little Horn

For I know the plans I have for you, declares YHWH, plans for welfare and not for evil, to give you a future and a hope (Jer 29:11).

I n some ways, I'm a pretty negative person. If someone asks me how it is to have a newborn baby in the home, I'll probably say, "Oh, it's awful!" Now, the fact is, a few years ago (when I first wrote this lesson) we had a baby in the house, and it was not awful; it was actually quite wonderful. But there were some negative aspects, like sleepless nights in the first few months. When someone tells me they're going to have a baby, my mind tends to go toward all the bad aspects. I figure everyone else is congratulating them and telling them how wonderful it's going to be, so they don't need me for that. They need a reality check. I do remember thinking when my wife, Jodi, and I were about three or four weeks into parenthood for the first time, "Why didn't anyone warn me?!" So I feel it's my job to warn expecting parents.

When I'm anticipating some event, I like to run through the worst-case scenarios and try to prepare myself for what might happen. When I'm going to get on a long overseas flight, I always think about how terrible it's going to be. The first time I went on a 15-hour flight, I wasn't prepared. I hadn't quite thought about how long fifteen hours is to spend on an airplane in coach. You watch three movies, and then you still have about ten hours left. It's awful! So that's the way I think now, to gear myself up for the flight.

These are minor things. Some things are a lot worse, and it's hard to gear up for them, but it's still helpful to know what's coming. Daniel 8 is a worst-case scenario kind of chapter, and it's much worse than being on a long flight or some sleepless nights with a newborn baby. There's a situation that's going to come on God's people, and it's going to be bad, but it's not going to last forever. The proper response is faith.

Daniel 8, which switches back to Hebrew after several chapters in Aramaic, is another chapter, like Daniel 7, in which animals represent kingdoms. This time, we only have two kingdoms, and those kingdoms are actually named in the text: the kingdom of the Medes and Persians and the kingdom of the Greeks. Readers of Daniel already know that Belshazzar—in whose reign this vision is given to Daniel (8:1)—is the last king of Babylon and that his kingdom will be replaced by the kingdom of the Medes and Persians (5:24–31). In Daniel 8, there's also another little horn, just like in Daniel 7, and it's this little horn that causes all the trouble. God describes the terrible situation for His people so that they know that this little horn didn't take God by surprise.

The Setup

A couple years after Daniel's dream of the four beasts and the son of man (cf. 7:1; 8:1), Daniel again had a vision of beasts, this time a ram and a goat. Daniel doesn't call this one a dream, but he does seem to say that both Chapter 7 and Chapter 8 are the same sort of thing (a vision; 8:1), so maybe we're supposed to understand that he's dreaming here as well. In the vision, Daniel says that he found himself in the city of Susa.[1] I take that to mean that he's not really, physically, in Susa, though some interpreters have thought so (e.g., Josephus, *Antiquities of the Jews* 10.269). Daniel had been taken to Babylon by Nebuchadnezzar and he had remained based there at least through the reign of Belshazzar (cf. 5:7), as far as we know. There is no mention that he moved to another city, though we can't rule it out. I assume, then, that he is in Babylon for this vision. According to Google Maps, Susa (Shush) would be about a 6-hour drive by car from Babylon (something like 300 miles).

Map 8.1 "The Drive from Babylon to Susa (via Google Maps)".

IT SEEMS that in the mid-sixth century BC (the time of the Jewish exile in Babylon) Susa was not a very important city. It was the capital of Elam, and Elam was incorporated at this time into the Median empire. Around 540 BC, Cyrus the Great, king of Persia, would incorporate into his burgeoning empire both Media and Elam (and most of the rest of the Near East). With

---

1. On Susa, see Prudence O. Harper, Joan Aruz, and Françoise Tallon, eds., *The Royal City of Susa: Ancient Near Eastern Treasures in the Louvre* (New York: Metropolitan Museum of Art, 1992).

the reign of Darius the Great (not Darius the Mede!), beginning about 521 BC, the city of Susa became one of the capitals of the Persian Empire.[2] Susa provides the setting for the book of Esther, and the book of Nehemiah starts in Susa.

The Vision

There's a ram with two long horns (8:3–4), and then a goat from the west with one big horn (8:5). The goat kills the ram, and then the goat's big horn is broken off and replaced by four horns (8:6–8). And then a little horn comes up and wreaks havoc on the beautiful land for 2300 mornings and evenings (8:9–14).

Then the angel Gabriel—looking like a man (8:15–16)—is told to interpret the vision for Daniel. (Who told him to do this? Michael the archangel? God? Both answers were ancient Jewish traditions.)[3] He identifies the ram as the Medes and the Persians and the goat as the Greeks. The big horn on the goat is the first Greek king (8:21), Alexander the Great (not actually named). And then Gabriel talks more about the little horn.

But before we can locate this section historically, we need to review some history.

A Little History Lesson

The Babylonian Empire was rather short-lived at only about 70 years.[4] We could mark the transition from the Assyrian Empire to the Babylonian Empire at the overthrow of the Assyrian

---

2. Lloyd Llewellyn-Jones describes Susa as the chief administrative center of the Persian empire under Darius I; see *Persians: The Age of Great Kings* (New York: Basic, 2022), 137–38.

3. See the discussion in Jay Braverman, *Jerome's Commentary on Daniel: A Study of Comparative Jewish and Christian Interpretations of the Hebrew Bible* (Washington, D.C.: The Catholic Biblical Association of America, 1978), 95–96.

4. I am of course talking about the neo-Babylonian Empire in the mid-first millennium BC. An older Babylonian Empire associated with Hammurabi had existed in the early-second millennium BC.

capital of Nineveh in 612 BC, and the conquest of the city of
Babylon by Cyrus the Great happened in 539 BC, so that's 73
years. In contrast, the Assyrian Empire lasted more than a
century, and the Persian Empire would last about two centuries.

Daniel's vision involves two empires, and we actually know
for sure which empires they are because Gabriel tells us (8:20–
21). But there is a complication: the first of the empires is a
double-empire, combining Media and Persia. The second empire
is the Greek one, not founded by Alexander the Great but
enlarged by him. We are certainly more familiar with the Greek
empire, or at least with Alexander, and Daniel's vision focuses
more on that empire, as well. So here we'll spend a little more
time talking about the Greeks, but first came the Persians.

MAP 8.2 "The Province of Fars (highlighted; via Google Maps)".

CYRUS WAS king of a city called Anshan in Persia, modern Fars
in southwestern Iran (see Map 8.2). At this point, there was
already a kingdom of Media, simultaneous with Babylon and

bigger in geography though maybe not as powerful.[5] The Median Empire—perhaps "empire" is too grandiose a term, despite the misleading account in Herodotus (*Histories* 1.95–130); Christopher Tuplin suggests "hegemony" or "domination"— was ruled by Cyrus' maternal grandfather.[6] The Persians were under Median domination until Cyrus conquered his grandfather's kingdom around 550 BC.[7] A decade later, he overcame Babylon and was the undisputed ruler of the entire Near East.[8] In Daniel's vision, the ram has two long horns, and the longer one came up second (8:3). The angel tells Daniel: "these are the kings of Media and Persia" (8:20). The vision connects Media and Persia (as does Daniel 6:8, 12, 15) as one animal, but also keeps them separate (two horns). The second horn that ends up being longer must be Cyrus, or Persia, as the bigger and more powerful, and newer, of the two kingdoms.

---

5. For a modern account, see Matt Waters, *Ancient Persia: A Concise History of the Achaemenid Empire, 550–330 BCE* (Cambridge: Cambridge University Press, 2014), 31–34, 38–39, though reading Herodotus (1.96–106) is more fun (and probably misleading).

6. See Herodotus 1.91. Christopher Tuplin, "Medes in Media, Mesopotamia, and Anatolia: Empire, Hegemony, Domination or Illusion?" *Ancient East & West* 3 (2004): 223–51. On Cyrus, see Matt Waters, *King of the World: The Life of Cyrus the Great* (Oxford: Oxford University Press, 2022). Ancient Greeks recognized that the Medes were very closely related to the Persians; see, e.g., Herodotus, *Histories* 9.43; Aeschylus, *The Persians*, line 238. See also Christopher Tuplin, "Persians as Medes," in *Achaemenid History*, vol. 8: *Continuity and Change*, ed. Heleen Sancisi Weerdenburg, Amélie Kuhrt, and Margaret Cool Root (Leiden: Netherlands Instituut voor het Nabije Oosten, 1994), 235–56.

7. You might think it rather unfriendly of Cyrus to conquer his grandfather's kingdom. According to Herodotus, this grandfather had tried to kill Cyrus as a baby, a rather unfriendly action in itself. For Herodotus' account of the birth of Cyrus and his rise to power over Persia and the Medes, see the *Histories* 1.107–30.

8. The *Nabonidus Chronicle* (ANET 306) and the *Cyrus Cylinder* (ANET 315–16) describe the peaceful entrance of Cyrus into Babylon, but Herodotus (*Histories* 1.186–200) narrates a battle.

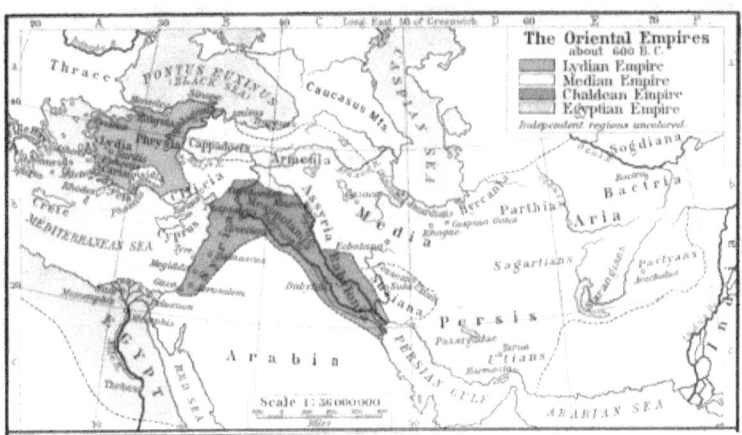

Map 8.3 "Median Empire (via Wikimedia Commons)"[9]

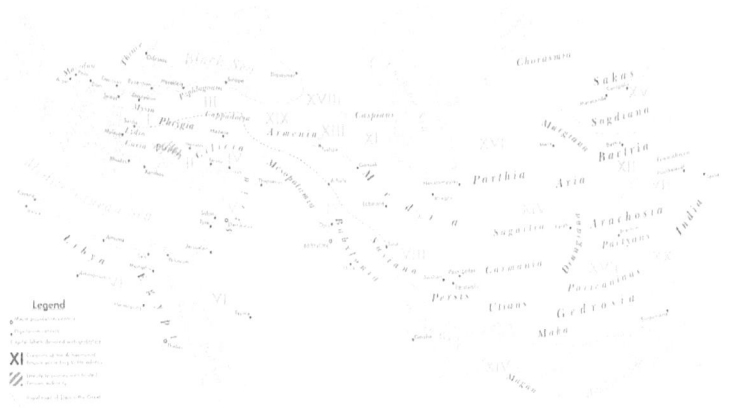

MAP 8.4: "Achaemenid Empire 500 BCE (via Wikimedia Commons)"[10]

---

9. https://commons.wikimedia.org/wiki/File:Median_Empire.jpg
10. https://commons.wikimedia.org/wiki/File:Achaemenid_Empire_500_BCE.jpg

Image 8.1: "Cyrus Cylinder (via Wikimedia Commons)"[11]

AFTER TWO HUNDRED YEARS, the Persian Empire was still going strong, but an ambitious 20-year-old Macedonian prince had his mind set on conquering the world, which meant heading East and pitching battle against the venerable, old Persian Empire. Alexander is, of course, the great horn on the goat (8:5) that ended up getting broken (8:8).[12] Once Alexander had won every battle from Macedon to India, his troops—tired of fighting and homesick—compelled him to turn west.[13] They got as far as Babylon, Daniel's own adopted home, where Alexander died in 323 BC, before his 33rd birthday, leaving his young, Persian wife Roxane nearly nine months pregnant. Without a clear successor, things devolved quickly. Here we have the wars of the diadochi. *Diadochus* is a Greek word for successor, and *diadochi* is plural, successors. The word refers to the generals and friends of Alexander who vied for power in the wake of the king's death.

---

11. https://commons.wikimedia.org/wiki/File:Cyrus_Cylinder.jpg.

12. For a collection of ancient sources on Alexander, see Waldemar Heckel and J. C. Yardley, *Alexander the Great: Historical Sources in Translation* (Malden, MA: Blackwell, 2004).

13. On the so-called Mutiny at the Hyphasis River, see the account of Quintus Curtius Rufus 9.2.1–3.20, in Heckel and Yardley, *Alexander*, 259–62. Another account is in Justin's *Epitome* 12.8.10–17; see *Epitome of the Philippic History of Pompeius Trogus*, trans. J. C. Yardley (Atlanta: Scholars Press, 1994), 116. See also Arrian, *Anabasis* 5.28–29.

The wars of the diadochi lasted for decades with many ups and downs for everyone.[14]

There weren't really four diadochi or four Hellenistic kingdoms. Well, maybe, but not really. Sometimes people say there were four because there are four horns in Daniel's vision that rise up in place of the big horn on the goat (8:8), and these four new horns are interpreted by the angel as representing four kingdoms (8:22). Some scholars—it seems to me—force the evidence to fit a literal interpretation of this statement, but the complicated history of the period makes it difficult to identify four specific kingdoms arising from Alexander's conquests as worthy candidates for the official four Hellenistic kingdoms. After the dust settled—whether you think of that dust settling after the Battle of Ipsus in 301 BC or after the Battle of Corupedium in 281 BC —there were two or three kingdoms associated with the diadochi. So, once again, I think the number four in the vision of Daniel has misled some people. We don't need to take it literally; like much of apocalyptic literature, it's figurative. This same sort of thing happens again later at 11:4, where the upshot is that Alexander's empire "is broken and divided toward the four winds of heaven." This business about his empire going in four pieces or in four directions I think simply means that it does not stay intact, in which case there's no problem in assuming the vision does not intend for us to think about four specific kingdoms.[15]

---

14. For an ancient account, see Justin, mentioned in the previous footnote. For a modern account, there are many options, but see, e.g., Robin Waterfield, *Dividing the Spoils: The War for Alexander the Great's Empire* (Oxford: Oxford University Press, 2011). I have briefly described these events in my academic article mentioned in the next note.

15. See Edmon L. Gallagher, "Daniel and the Diadochi," *Journal of Biblical Literature* 141 (2022): 301–16.

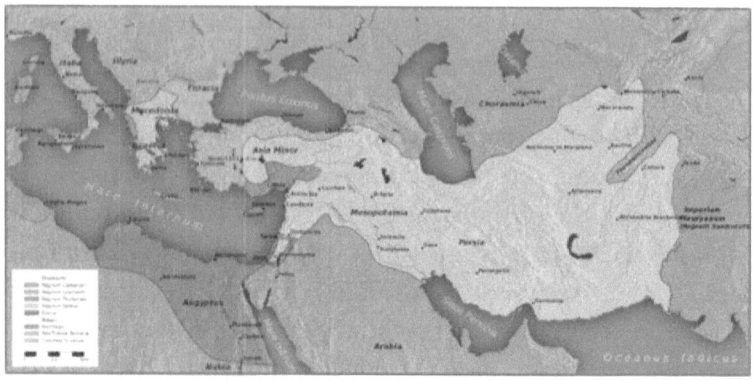

Map 8.5: "The Kingdoms of the Diadochi (via Wikimedia Commons)"[16]

IN FACT, for the history of the Jews, we really only care about two of these kingdoms of the diadochi, the two most prominent ones, that of Ptolemy in Egypt and Seleucus in most of the territory of the old Persian Empire. Both of these kingdoms take center stage again in Daniel 11, but here in Daniel 8, it's really Seleucus that we care about. It's one of his descendants that's the little horn. That would be the king named Antiochus IV Epiphanes, who ruled 175–164 BC over a territory that included Judah. It's this period that gives us the Maccabean Revolt, and our main sources for these events are the two books of Maccabees that are a part of the deuterocanonical books (or the apocrypha) in the Roman Catholic Bible.

Let me briefly tell you about this period of Jewish history. According to 2 Maccabees, there were some Jews who wanted to modernize Jerusalem (i.e., make it a hip Greek city) and update Jewish culture (stop following all those antiquated biblical laws). Such a plan sounded good to the Greek king Antiochus. And then some fighting over the priesthood led Antiochus to think

---

16. https://commons.wikimedia.org/wiki/File:Diadochi_LA.svg.

that there was a rebellion in Jerusalem. These factors and others combined to cause Antiochus to do something unprecedented: he basically outlawed traditional Jewish religion. He tried to force Jews to eat pork (2 Macc 6–7). He outlawed circumcision (1 Macc 1:48). He tried to force people to profane the Sabbath (1:43, 45). He destroyed Torah scrolls and killed anyone found with a copy (1:56–57). The temple in Jerusalem he rededicated to Zeus rather than the Jewish God (2 Macc 6:2). And he sacrificed swine (1 Macc 1:47). Understandably, all this angered some Jews very much, and some of them rebelled against their Greek overlords, and these Jewish rebels were called the Maccabees. Two or three years of fighting saw them win back control of the temple, and their purification of the temple gave birth to a new holiday, Hanukkah (1 Macc 4:37–59; 2 Macc 10:1–8).

It's not hard to see why Daniel's vision would represent Antiochus as the little horn that "shall cause fearful destruction" (8:24).

The Period of Wrath

The point of this vision, it seems to me, is that there will be a period of wrath (8:19)—wrath, yes, but just for a period.

When is this supposed to happen? The word "end" appears twice in this chapter, in two different phrases (8:17, 19). The Hebrew word for "end" is *qēts* (or *qēṣ*; קץ), which appears sixty-seven times in the Hebrew Bible, and fifteen times in Daniel—by far the most in the Bible. (Second place goes to Ezekiel, with nine occurrences of *qēts*.) All fifteen appearances of *qēts* in Daniel come in chapters 8–12.[17]

Our initial instinct would be to think that "the time of the end" (8:17) and "the appointed time of the end" (8:19)—the time

---

17. 8:17, 19; 9:26 twice; 11:6, 13, 27, 35, 40, 45; 12:4, 6, 9, 13 twice. See John J. Collins, "The Meaning of 'the End' in the Book of Daniel," in *Of Scribes and Scrolls: Studies on the Hebrew Bible, Intertestamental Judaism, and Christian Origins*, ed. H. W. Attridge et al. (Lanham, MD: University Press of America, 1990), 91–98.

when this vision of the ram and goat is supposed to be fulfilled—must be talking about the end of the world, except that, in our modern period, the dominant empires of Persia and Greece have been gone for a long time. If this vision does describe the end of the world, maybe the Little Horn is the Antichrist. That view is pretty popular and ancient (Jerome insists on this idea), but it's hard to see how the original readers of the text would have thought that way. Maybe we're not supposed to connect this vision with the end of the world. In fact, sometimes in Daniel the word *qēts* cannot be referring to the end of the world or the end of time, because after the *qēts*, things continue to happen in this world, in this time. For instance, in chapter 11: "After some years they shall make an alliance, and the daughter of the king of the south shall come to the king of the north to make an agreement" (Dan 11:6). That phrase "after some years" in Hebrew uses the word *qēts* and could be translated, "at the end of years," but it obviously doesn't refer to the absolute end of all years (the end of time) because history keeps going in chapter 11. So also at 11:13, where English translations again have the phrase "after some years," the Hebrew could more literally be translated "at the end of times." Maybe it would help us to think of *qēts* as "limit," like some sort of divinely preordained limit to a period of history. God is going to allow something to happen until it reaches its limit, at which point things are going to change. In her commentary on Daniel, Carol Newsom points to Habakkuk 2:3, which also uses *qēts* in the sense of a preordained limit to a historical period (in this case, Babylonian dominance).[18]

All that to say that even though we might initially think that this vision is about the end of time, that's probably not what Gabriel means. Rather, it's for the "time of the end," the foreordained limit to some period of history, after which history—or time, or the world—will continue.

---

18. Carol A. Newsom and Brennan W. Breed, *Daniel*, Old Testament Library (Louisville: WJK, 2014), 269.

The period of history that has a foreordained end is called "a period of wrath" (8:19). The vision given to Daniel "will take place later in the period of wrath; for it refers to the appointed time of the end" ... of the period of wrath. Daniel is actually living during the period of wrath, for the Babylonian exile is apparently the start of it. The period of wrath is probably the same thing as the period during which the Gentile kingdoms—the kingdoms of Nebuchadnezzar's statue in Daniel 2 and the four beasts in Daniel 7—dominate God's people.

Whose wrath? Maybe the Gentiles' wrath, or the wrath of Antiochus Epiphanes, but probably not. When you're reading the Bible and you hear about wrath, who do you think of? God, of course, and that's probably the case here. This is a period of God's wrath. Think about this other verse from another apocalyptic prophet.

> Then the angel of YHWH said, "O YHWH of hosts, how long will you withhold mercy from Jerusalem and the cities of Judah, with which you have been angry these seventy years?" (Zech 1:12).

Zechariah is talking about the seventy years of Babylonian exile as a period of God's wrath. Gabriel reveals to Daniel that it's going to last longer than just those seventy years (as he will also do in the next chapter), but it's not going to last forever. Why is God angry? Well, why do you think? It's because of sin. God's people ignored Him, He got angry and sent them into exile. They are enduring the period of His wrath, which is going to get worse before it gets better. The Gentile kingdoms themselves are going to transgress their mandate from God, and when they have filled up the measure of their sins (8:23; cf. Gen 15:16), God will overthrow them and again act in mercy for His people.

This is all supposed to take 2300 evenings and mornings (8:14). Does that mean 1150 evenings and 1150 mornings, so that the total of 2300 evenings and mornings is actually 1150 days (= a

little over three years)? Or is it supposed to be 2300 days (=
somewhat over six years)? Commentators disagree, but if we're
talking about the defilement of the temple during the days of
Antiochus IV Epiphanes, then the chronology would work
better if it were a little over three years (which is how long the
temple was defiled according to 1 Maccabees).[19] Why talk about
evenings and mornings rather than just days? Because sacrifice
was supposed to be offered evenings and mornings.

Lamenting and Working

It's going to get worse before it gets better. That's Gabriel's
message to Daniel, and it's a message we often need to hear. We
like to remind ourselves of Jeremiah 29:11, that God has plans for
our welfare and not for our harm, and that is, of course, true, but
that verse does not exhaust the truth that God wants us to know.
In fact, sometimes God has plans for our harm—or, not for our
harm so much as for our discomfort. All of God's plans for us
intend ultimately to result in our good, but that doesn't mean
we'll enjoy them all. Sometimes, in God's mysterious wisdom, He
sees fit to bring us pain. That's what has happened to Jeremiah's
readers in Jeremiah 29; that is the reason the prophet needs to
reassure his readers that God does plan for their welfare, because
these readers are sitting in exile, having experienced a portion (a
painful portion) of God's plans.

    The little horn in Daniel 8 is going to succeed in causing
destruction (8:24). He's going to prosper in his evil (8:12). That is
a hard message to hear, and Daniel doesn't understand it (8:27).
We might not understand it either.

    Ultimately God's plans for us are for our welfare and not for
our harm. But we will experience pain before we arrive at that

---

19. 1 Maccabees 1:54, 59; 4:52–53. See also Josephus, *Antiquities of the Jews* 12.320–
21. On the other hand, 2 Maccabees 10:3 says that the temple was defiled for two
years.

ultimate period of welfare. In some ways, we still (today, in the twenty-first century) endure a continuation of the period of wrath. We still witness domination by ungodly people. Even a very brief listing of a few of the world's massive problems can make your head spin: violence, poverty, lack of clean water, children without homes, and trafficking. Trying to untangle just one of those issues is too big for us. It can lead us to despair.

Here's what Daniel did when he saw this vision of the period of wrath. "So I, Daniel, was overcome and lay sick for some days; then I arose and went about the king's business. But I was dismayed by the vision and did not understand it" (8:27). We can sympathize with seeing such a vision and needing to lie down for some days. Eventually, Daniel got up.

The narrator in the novel *The Silver Chair* puts it this way: "Crying is all right in its way while it lasts. But you have to stop sooner or later, and then you still have to decide what to do."[20] What can Daniel do about the massive problem that has just been revealed to him? He can't do much. He needs to understand that it is not his responsibility to solve that problem. He couldn't possibly. But he can lament, and he can work. He can do the task right in front of him.

I think often about this couple I saw in Haiti. I was in a van driving outside Port-au-Prince, and I looked out the window and saw a woman sweeping the road, and a man behind her shoveling dirt into a wheelbarrow. I wonder what they thought they could accomplish. Certainly, they had no chance of cleaning up the streets of Haiti; they could not possibly solve the problem. But they could clean up their little area. They could do what was right in front of them. When Sally and her brother were standing there, mouths agape, staring at the enormous mess that the Cat in the Hat had made in their house, the voice of wisdom came from their fish, who advised them, "Do something!"

---

20. C. S. Lewis, *The Silver Chair*, The Chronicles of Narnia (New York: Harper-Collins, 1953), 18.

There is a time for lamentation. And there is a time for work. (Are the Byrds playing in your head, now?) Solving the massive problems of the world is up to God, and He will solve them, one way or another. Our job is to be faithful—to Him, and to the task right in front of us.

Discussion Questions

- Why do you think God reveals these events to Daniel? What is the use of revealing these events in this way?
- What do you make of the references to "the end" in this chapter? The end of what?
- Here again (as in Daniel 7) we learn about a little horn that causes trouble. What kind of trouble does this little horn cause? Why does God allow the little horn to have such success?
- This chapter talks about a period of wrath. Do you think you are living through a period of wrath? Do you think the society in which you live is enduring a period of wrath? How so?
- Does Daniel's response to this vision (verse 27) resonate with you? Have you responded to events in your life in a similar fashion?

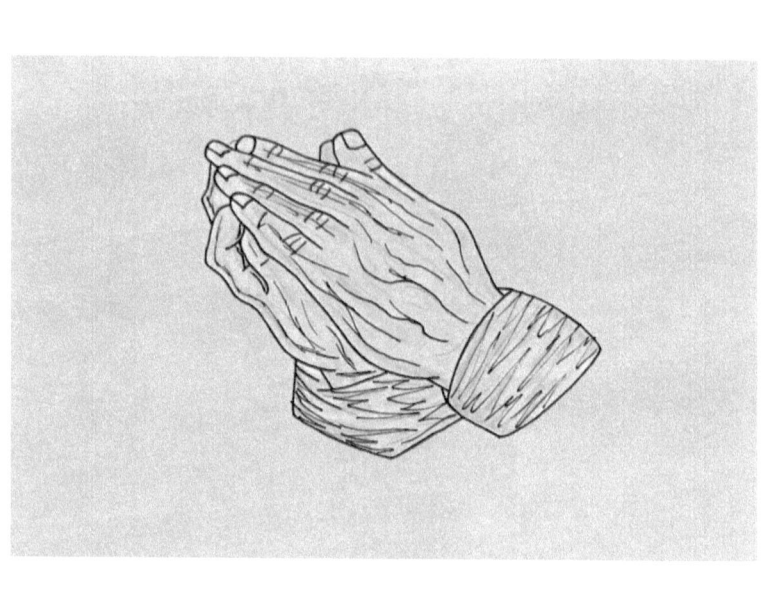

Chapter 9
Daniel's Prayer and the Seventy Weeks

H ere we reach the most difficult chapter in the book of Daniel, thanks to the last four verses, the Prophecy of the Seventy Weeks. In this chapter, Daniel prays about his sin and the sin of his people, and then Gabriel the angel returns and seemingly reveals a timetable for some things to happen. The timetable is so obscure, so difficult to interpret, that it has inspired many different interpretations, and I don't know whether any of them are correct. But that doesn't make the interpretation of the chapter hopeless. God has given us Daniel 9 for our edification, and we can understand it—or, at least, some things about it.

What can we say about this chapter? God is going to take care of sin. He's going to do it on His timetable. Also, some bad things are going to happen. When will it all happen? I don't know, but God does.

The Seventy Years of Exile

Our chapter starts with Daniel reading the words of another prophet: "I, Daniel, perceived in the books the number of years that, according to the word of YHWH to the prophet Jeremiah, must be fulfilled for the devastation of Jerusalem, namely, seventy years" (Dan 9:2).[1] The number 70 years, as the timespan of the exile, comes up a couple of times in the book of Jeremiah. First, Jeremiah announces the coming destruction to the inhabitants of Jerusalem.

> This whole land shall become a ruin and a waste, and these nations shall serve the king of Babylon seventy years. Then after seventy years are completed, I will punish the king of Babylon and that nation, the land of the Chaldeans, for their iniquity, says YHWH, making the land an everlasting waste (Jer 25:11–12).

Later, Jeremiah writes a letter to the people who had already been exiled to Babylon, encouraging them to "build houses and live in them; plant gardens and eat what they produce" (Jer 29:5) —in other words, to recognize that they would spend the rest of their lives in Babylon. The exile would not be brief. "For thus says YHWH: Only when Babylon's seventy years are completed will I visit you, and I will fulfill to you my promise to bring you back to this place" (Jer 29:10).

The exile didn't last precisely seventy years, but it's hard to know exactly how long it did last. It depends on what date you think marks the beginning of the exile.[2] There were, in fact, multiple waves of exile. The last chapter of the book of Jeremiah

---

1. Why do we read about "books" here in Daniel? Maybe it just means the sacred books, among which was the book of Jeremiah. But it could also refer to multiple "books" of Jeremiah, since the prophet sent a "book" (or letter) to the exiles (29:1), and he also wrote another "book" about the destruction of Jerusalem (25:13). See Michael Segal, "The Chronological Conception of the Persian Period in Daniel 9," *Journal of Ancient Judaism* 2 (2011): 283–303, at 291. Or, it may be that the literary work we know as the "Book of Jeremiah" existed across a number of papyrus scrolls, in accordance with the argument of Nathan Mastnjak, *Before the Scrolls: A Material Approach to Israel's Prophetic Library* (Oxford: Oxford University Press, 2023).

2. As noted in the fifth by Theodoret of Cyrus, *Commentary on Daniel*, trans. Robert C. Hill (Atlanta: SBL, 2006), 223–29.

mentions three waves: one in the seventh year of Nebuchadnezzar, 597 BC (Jer 52:28), one in his eighteenth year, 586 BC (52:29),
and another in his twenty-third year, 581 BC (Jer 52:30). The
second wave (586 BC) is when the temple was destroyed and the
Davidic monarchy came to an end (2 Kgs 25:8–26). The first wave
(597 BC) is when King Jehoiachin was taken to Babylon (2 Kgs
24:8–20) and his uncle, (who became known as) Zedekiah,
started to reign in Judah. It is from this event, the exile of
Jehoiachin, that, for example, Ezekiel's prophecies are dated (see
Ezek 1:2). The exile came to an end when Cyrus the Great, king
of Persia, conquered Babylon and allowed the various peoples to
return to their ancestral lands.[3] The year was 539 or 538 BC.
According to Ezra 1:1, this was the moment to which Jeremiah
had been pointing in his predicting the end of the exile (see also
2 Chron 36:22).[4] An exile that starts in 597 BC and ends in 538
BC gets us only to about sixty years.

Nevertheless, we have a couple of retrospective verses (not
predictions, like in Jeremiah) claiming that the exile did last
seventy years. The prophet Zechariah, living in the early days of
the Persian period, mentions that God had been angry with his
people "these seventy years" (Zech 1:12). He seems to think that
the construction of the Second Temple, dedicated in 516 BC (cf.
Ezra 6:15), marked the end of the period of God's wrath.
Perhaps, then, Zechariah would say that the exile did last
precisely seventy years, the length of time between the destruction of the temple in 586 BC and its rededication in 516 BC.

According to 2 Chronicles, the exile lasted "until the land
had made up for its sabbaths" (2 Chron 36:21), presumably the

---

3. The Cyrus Cylinder, discovered in Babylon, mentions this policy of Cyrus,
but not in relation to the Jews specifically. See the translation of line 32 at https://
www.livius.org/sources/content/cyrus-cylinder/.

4. In some ways, Ezra (9:8–9) and Nehemiah (9:36–37) and later Jewish authors
imagined the exile as continuing past the time of the events described in the first
chapter of Ezra. See N. T. Wright, *The New Testament and the People of God* (Minneapolis: Fortress, 1992), 268–72; James Seung-Hyun Lee, *Reimagining Exile in
Daniel: A Literary-Historical Study* (Tübingen: Mohr Siebeck, 2023).

sabbatical years (cf. Lev 25:1–7) that had been ignored by the Israelites. The verse continues: "All the days that it lay desolate it kept sabbath, to fulfill seventy years." This had all been promised by God through Moses in the book of Leviticus when God warned that exile would allow the land to "enjoy its sabbath years as long as it lies desolate. ... As long as it lies desolate, it shall have the rest it did not have on your sabbaths when you were living on it" (Lev 25:34–35). But 2 Chronicles does not tell us how to count the seventy years of exile.

The book of Daniel might have something to say about this issue. The whole book begins by mentioning an otherwise unknown time of exile: "In the third year of the reign of King Jehoiakim of Judah, King Nebuchadnezzar of Babylon came to Jerusalem and besieged it" (Dan 1:1). This is the moment when Daniel and his three friends were captured and transported to Babylon. The third year of Jehoiakim would be about 606 BC. As I mentioned, this exile is otherwise unattested, but counting the exile from 606 BC would get us pretty close to seventy years at the time of Cyrus's conquest to Babylon in 539 BC.

I do wonder, though, whether all this calculating misses Jeremiah's point. Maybe "seventy" wasn't intended to be a precise number, but was intended to be a round number that signaled two realities: (1) the people transported to Babylon by Nebuchadnezzar would never see their homeland again; they would die in exile; and (2) a later generation of Jewish people in the not-too-distant future would return to their ancestral homeland. If this is what the number "seventy" communicates, rather than a literal number, then it wouldn't really matter if the exile actually lasted fifty years or a hundred years; those periods would still be consistent with the point that Jeremiah wanted to make.

We recognize that the Bible sometimes uses numbers in this way, schematically rather than literally. "The days of our life are seventy years, or perhaps eighty, if we are strong" (Ps 90:10). There is no need for me to demonstrate that the human lifespan varies quite widely and that this verse does not deny such variety.

The idea that Jeremiah did not intend his "seventy years" as a precise reckoning may find support in literature contemporary with the prophet. According to scholar Gary A. Anderson, "a seventy-year period of destruction was something of a commonplace in the ancient Near East."[5] I believe, also, that the references to seventy years in Zechariah and 2 Chronicles could cohere with this schematic reading of Jeremiah's number; maybe they both understand the number as somewhat imprecise. Note that this view is different from saying that the Jeremiah's seventy years is symbolic, along the lines of Augustine: "the seventy years of Jeremiah may be understood spiritually as the whole of the time during which the church is among foreigners."[6]

Daniel (I mean the person, not the book) apparently did not understand the number as symbolic, or not at first, anyway. This chapter, Daniel 9, is dated to "the first year of Darius son of Ahasuerus, by birth a Mede" (9:1). According to the book of Daniel, Darius the Mede was the king who took control of the city of Babylon following the death of Babylon's last king, Belshazzar (Dan 5:30–31). This marked the end of the Neo-Babylonian Empire, and we should probably imagine that Daniel was wondering whether the exile would soon be over. So he got out his copy of Jeremiah and studied the oracles, trying to figure out when the predicted time period would be accomplished.

Daniel's Prayer

If Daniel had been looking at the letter that Jeremiah sent to the exiles (maybe we should imagine that Daniel was himself one of the recipients of this letter), then he would have read the following words immediately after the prediction of the seventy years.

5. Gary A. Anderson, *Sin: A History* (New Haven, CT: Yale University Press, 2009), 77.
6. Augustine, *On Christian Teaching* 3.35.51.121, trans. R. P. H. Green, Oxford World's Classics (Oxford: Oxford University Press, 1997), 96.

For surely I know the plans I have for you, says YHWH, plans
for your welfare and not for harm, to give you a future with
hope. Then when you call upon me and come and pray to me, I
will hear you. When you search for me, you will find me; if you
seek me with all your heart, I will let you find me, says YHWH,
and I will restore your fortunes and gather you from all the
nations and all the places where I have driven you, says
YHWH, and I will bring you back to the place from which I
sent you into exile (Jer 29:11–14).

The message essentially is: "After seventy years in exile, if you
seek me, I will restore you to your homeland." So Daniel seeks
God. Why does Daniel pray? Most basically, he prays because
that's what Jeremiah told the exiles to do in this situation.
(Remember also what Solomon prayed in 1 Kings 8:46–53,
mentioned earlier in chapter 6.) But also Daniel prays because he
is calling on God to keep His promises. Not that he doubted
that God would fulfill His promises, but … as Jerome said many
centuries ago, the certainty of God's promises "did not render
Daniel careless, but rather encouraged him to pray that God
might through his supplications fulfill that which He had
graciously promised."[7] But Daniel prays also because he is not
sure that the exile has lasted long enough to purify God's people
of sin.

Daniel prays a confessional prayer, confessing sin. What sin
has Daniel committed? While we should not imagine that
Daniel is sinless, you can read the stories in Daniel 1–6 and never
find a moment when Daniel messed up, when he made a
mistake, when he wavered in his faithfulness to God. I doubt
that the prayer of Daniel 9 is presented to us so that we will
think that Daniel himself participated in the sins that brought

---

7. Jerome, *Commentary on Daniel*, trans. Gleason L. Archer (Grand Rapids:
Baker, 1958), 90.

about the exile—the idolatry and such. If we know anything about Daniel, he was no idolator.

So what can he mean by praying, "we have sinned and done wrong, acted wickedly and rebelled, turning aside from your commandments and ordinances" (Dan 9:5). He confesses the sin of his people, and he is one of his people. To some degree, he shares the guilt—and he certainly shares the punishment—that led to the exile.

There has been a lot of talk in America over the past several years, maybe decades, about societal evil, systemic ills. Take racism: could a system—government, industry, education, whatever—have rules in place that favor one group over another? Might those rules have been put in place decades ago by people who were avowed racists? And might later generations who have been trained to regard racism as unacceptable and revolting still benefit or suffer, as the case may be, from these older rules? Perhaps someone of that later generation who feels no prejudice in his or her heart against another group—perhaps that person will still benefit from the system put in place to secure one race's advantage over another. Is such a person complicit in societal evil?

Or, when I look back on a previous generation and observe their actions, the sinfulness of which is so obvious to me, what should I pray? "Thank you, God, that I am not like them"? Or "God, be merciful to me, a sinner"? Reflecting on the sins of previous generations should probably prod us to wonder how later generations will think about us.

Let's go in a different direction. I have an iPhone sitting next to me as I type. I have no doubt that some evil went into the production of this iPhone. I'm not sure precisely what kind of evil, but I believe the Apple company gets some parts from China, and I believe the ruling government of China participates in a great deal of evil, and maybe even this very iPhone that I have has parts produced by child slave labor in China. It may very well be that the pious and righteous thing to do would be to avoid Apple products altogether, and maybe it is my own inner wickedness that tells me that such a stance would be pointless. Nevertheless, such a stance seems at least to border on being pointless, since Apple is not the only company that produces their products with the help of evil. How can I live in modern America and avoid such products? Aren't they all around me? I guess I could live like the Amish, but I'm not confident that would do the trick.

The fact is, as long as we live in this world, we will be surrounded by evil, and we will be influenced by it, and we will sometimes benefit from it and refuse to forgo those benefits. I think Daniel realized this about himself. He was a member of the royal family in Judah, after all. If anyone benefited from the general wickedness of Judean society, it was the royal family. And even in Babylon, the land of his captivity, Daniel benefited from his close relationship with brutal dictators. That's, of course, not to say that Daniel is basically wicked himself; it's only to say that none of us can maintain complete purity. And even when we try to live godly lives, we find sin accompanying us. Sometimes even the very deeds we do in order to glorify God—say, feeding the hungry—are themselves infected by sin; feeding the hungry is a good way to look righteous in front of others, after all (see Matt 6:1–18). It turns out that "we have all become like one who is unclean, and all our righteous deeds are like a filthy cloth" (Isa 64:6).

Some sins are bigger than just one person; some sins are societal—either from the way people who do not directly participate in the sin still support those who do in unknowing ways, or from the failure of people to fight against the sin that they know is tearing people down. To what extent do we share some complicity in the sins of materialism, or racism, or abortion, or sex trafficking, or chemical addictions?

> Let us be clear about this. Grace certainly frees individual believers from the guilt of national, familial, and personal sin.

The sins of our history and context do not keep us from individually enjoying the benefits of grace. And yet the benefits of grace should not keep individuals from confessing corporate responsibility for the sins of our families and culture. If I am so swept into a culture of materialism that I do not see or fight against the impoverishment of the disadvantaged, then I need to confess my personal sin. In addition, if I see and object to the sin but still live in, and benefit from, the society driven by such aims, then my confession of our corporate sin is appropriate. If I find racism abhorrent but still have advantages from the slave-owning heritage of my family or the oppression-ignoring history of my church, then I should confess the sin of my family and ecclesiastical affiliations. If I personally find the sins of abortion, sex trafficking, and chemical addictions abhorrent but find my life entwined in a culture that promotes such evil, then I have a responsibility to confess *our* sin with the prayer that God would bring His mercy and power to bear upon all of these evils. Grace is great enough to cover all our sin—individual and corporate—but does not free us from responsibilities to confess both.[8]

There are a lot of people who major in defending themselves and condemning others. There is a place for self-defense and for condemnation—or, at least, rebuke—of others, but I don't want to major in those things. I want to major in recognizing my own faults and seeking God's mercy for myself and others.[9]

Gabriel's Message

In response to Daniel's prayer asking God to remove Israel's sin in light of the end of the promised seventy years of exile, God

---

8. Bryan Chapell, *The Gospel According to Daniel: A Christ-Centered Approach* (Grand Rapids: Baker, 2014), 160.
9. See for more Bonnie Kristian, "Confessing Complicity in Systemic Sin," *Christianity Today* (August 20, 2020).

sends the angel Gabriel to inform Daniel that God will indeed remove sin, but He has a different timetable in mind, not seventy years but seventy weeks. But the seventy weeks are divided up into three periods (7 weeks, 62 weeks, 1 week), or maybe only two periods (7 + 62 weeks = 69 weeks, and 1 week), and some other things are going to happen during these weeks beyond simply God's removal of sin. Gabriel's revelation is a little difficult to follow, but it seems to describe a period of suffering for God's people, an anointed person or two, and something called the abomination of desolation.

Let me say it again: this is a difficult passage.[10] I don't know what it all means. There are some passages in the Bible that are like arithmetic: 2 + 2 = 4. They seem pretty straightforward, easy to interpret. This is not one of those passages. Daniel 9 is not an arithmetic passage, it's a calculus passage. This is not the passage you come to when you're starting out in Bible study; this is one you get to after you've already been studying the Bible for some years. That prior study doesn't mean that you're going to understand this passage, but it will give you a basis for thinking about its meaning.

Let's start with something about which everyone seems to agree: in this passage "week" = "week of years," i.e., seven years. The idea that we might group time into seven-year periods is not that unusual in the Bible. Think about the sabbatical year, which —as we saw above—had some bearing on the length of time of the exile. There's also the jubilee year, which is the year after a series of seven sabbatical years, or, as Leviticus 25:8 puts it, seven sabbaths of years (an expression that sounds a lot like Dan 9:24). Other ancient Jewish writings sometimes counted time in generations rather than years, and they would group seven generations together and call it a week (of generations). Do you remember

---

10. Not everyone finds this passage difficult. The dispensationalist Charles Ryrie seems to think the passage is pretty clear and easy to interpret; see Charles C. Ryrie, *Dispensationalism*, 2d ed. (Chicago: Moody, 2007), 208. Needless to say, I do not find his interpretation at all compelling.

how Enoch was the seventh generation from Adam, a fact mentioned at Jude 14? The writing known as *1 Enoch* 93:3 represents Enoch as saying, "I was born the seventh in the first week."[11] The first week is the first seven generations. I just bring this up to show that sometimes in ancient Jewish literature, a week is not seven days.

If Daniel 9 is talking about 70 "weeks of years"—70 seven-year periods—then the total would be 490 years. But are we supposed to take this literally, as if God is giving us a timeline that we should calculate, or is 70 weeks more symbolic? Sometimes the Bible uses numbers symbolically: when Jesus says you should forgive someone not seven times but 77 times (Matt 18:22), nobody takes it literally, as if Jesus was putting a limit on our forgiveness (not above 77 times!), the exact opposite of the point He was making. In regard to Daniel 9, conservative Christians usually (at least, in my experience) have tried to take the 490 years literally, but there are problems with this approach. There are problems with any approach, and the issues are so complex we will take the passage verse-by-verse in a moment. I will say, though, that I lean toward the idea of taking the 70 weeks sorta symbolically, or at least as so complicated that God doesn't really intend for us readers of Daniel to calculate the period indicated by the 70 weeks.[12] (For more on this idea, see below in my discussion of verse 25.)

One more thing, though, before we begin the verse-by-verse examination: what does Gabriel expect us to think about the

---

11. For more on this, see Ed Gallagher, *The Gospel of Luke: Explorations in Christian Scripture* (Florence, AL: Heritage Christian Univesity Press, 2022), 82–89.

12. For a symbolic interpretation, see Edward J. Young, *The Prophecy of Daniel: A Commentary* (Grand Rapids: Eerdmans, 1949), 206; Jim McGuiggan, *The Book of Daniel* (Lubbock, TX: Montex, 1978), 188–204; C. F. Keil (d. 1888), *Biblical Commentary on the Book of Daniel* (repr.: Grand Rapids: Eerdmans, 1968). For a halfway symbolic view, see C. L. Seow, *Daniel* (Louisville: WJK, 2003), who feels that he can calculate the first 7 weeks (p. 148) but for the rest he says, "The years are symbolic and, at best, only approximate historical periods. They are probably not literal and precise years" (p. 149).

relationship between his 70 weeks and Jeremiah's 70 years? Some scholars think that Gabriel has come to tell Daniel that he has misunderstood Jeremiah, that in fact Jeremiah's prediction of a 70-year exile actually signified an exile that would last for 70 weeks of years.[13] Not everyone shares this idea, and I think it makes more sense to say that Gabriel brings a new revelation about a different period of time.[14] After all, the exile—at least in some ways—did come to an end in about 538 BC; some Jews did return to the land of Judah to rebuild the temple and reconstitute Jewish life in their ancestral land. I assume that those events constituted the end of exile that Jeremiah predicted. But, it turned out that the exile did not fix the sin problem of God's people. Gabriel revealed that God had a plan for that, too.

One more thing again: when you study this passage, you need to look at various translations. There are differences among them. Below we'll look at the KJV, NRSV, NASB, and maybe a few others.

Verse 24

Most translations of this verse are pretty close to each other. Gabriel tells Daniel about a period of seventy weeks in which several things are going to happen "for your people and your holy city."

- to finish the transgression
- to put an end to sin
- and to atone for iniquity
- to bring in everlasting righteousness

---

13. James C. VanderKam, *The Dead Sea Scrolls and the Bible* (Grand Rapids: Eerdmans, 2012), 28–30. See also Michael Fishbane, *Biblical Interpretation in Ancient Israel* (Oxford: Oxford University Press, 1985), 479–85.

14. See Segal, "Chronological Conception," who also cites the twelfth-century Jewish commentator Abraham Ibn Ezra as holding this position.

- to seal both vision and prophet (or prophecy = KJV, NASB)
- to anoint a most holy place (KJV: anoint the most Holy)

Verse 25

This verse presents some difficulties, and translations diverge in a couple of areas. Let me just quote the KJV, and then we'll talk about the main differences among the translations.

> Know therefore and understand, *that* from the going forth of the commandment to restore and to build Jerusalem unto the Messiah the Prince *shall be* seven weeks, and threescore and two weeks: the street shall be built again, and the wall, even in troublous times.

A first difficulty in this verse concerns the chronology. The period of 70 weeks from the previous verse is broken up into smaller chunks, and in our verse, a period of seven weeks is named, and also a period of 62 weeks. But do they go together or are they separate? In other words, are the seven weeks and the 62 weeks two different periods of time (NRSV, ESV, CEB, Scofield), or do they go together, basically just amounting to one big period of 69 weeks (KJV, NASB, NIV, CSB)?

A second area of difficulty has to do with the anointed one in this verse. Shall we render the Hebrew as "an anointed prince" (NRSV, ESV, CEB), or "the Messiah the Prince" (KJV, NASB, NIV, CSB)? The Hebrew phrase (*mashiaḥ nagid*, מָשִׁיחַ נָגִיד) could be rendered either way.

As for the first issue, the division of the weeks, the problem comes because this verse mentions a seven-week period and a 62-week period. According to one view, these are two different periods, and the seven-week period lasts from the going forth of the commandment to restore and rebuild Jerusalem until the time of an anointed prince (or, unto the Messiah the Prince), whereas the 62-week period is characterized by the elements mentioned next in the verse. According to another view, the two periods go together to make a 69-week period, which starts at the command to restore Jerusalem and ends with the anointed prince. We can see the different views by comparing English Bibles: for the NRSV (and similar translations), this first period of time will be seven weeks (49 years, perhaps), and then the 62 weeks (= 434 years?) marks the time when the city "shall be built again with streets and moat"; the KJV takes the other view (as indicated by the punctuation). Both reckonings are ancient: the traditional Hebrew text suggests that the 62 weeks should be counted separately from the first seven weeks, but the traditional Greek version (Theodotion) and the Latin Vulgate count the two periods together.[15]

In the modern period, the timing issue is related to the translation of an "anointed prince." If you think the anointed prince here is Jesus the Christ (Messiah), then you need a lot longer time than simply seven weeks (49 years) from the "decree to restore and rebuild Jerusalem." If that decree refers to Cyrus' decree mentioned at the very beginning of Ezra (539 BC), then seven weeks later (assuming a week = seven years) only gets us to about 490 BC, way before Jesus. We need more time, and counting the 62 weeks with the seven weeks would help. Then again, even if we put all these weeks together so that we count 69 weeks (= 463 years) from 539 BC, that still gets us only to about 76 BC, about a century too early (if we think that the calculation is supposed to end up at the crucifixion).

At this point, we've got several options.

• Maybe we should start the reckoning later. Maybe "the decree to restore and rebuild Jerusalem" is not Cyrus' decree but

---

15. Segal, "Chronological Conception," 293 n. 31. The Old Greek translation has no time indication in verse 25, but in verse 26 it confusingly mentions seven and 70 and 62 weeks.

rather some later decree. Maybe it refers to the permission granted to Nehemiah by the Persian king Artaxerxes in 444 BC to build the walls of Jerusalem. Calculating 69 weeks later gets us to about AD 19, definitely within the lifetime of Jesus and reasonably close to the crucifixion (about eleven or twelve years later). It's still not super precise, but it's not bad.

• Maybe we should not think that Jesus is the person called "an anointed prince." There were all kinds of "anointed" people. In fact, maybe this passage in Daniel talks about two different "anointed" people, one in verse 25, and a different one in verse 26, where we read that an anointed one is "cut off." This inter- pretation (two different anointed ones) would probably necessi- tate that we separate the seven weeks from the 62 weeks. After seven weeks, there's going to be an anointed one, who is also called a prince, and then 62 weeks later, there's going to be another anointed one. This second anointed one is not called a prince, though the word "prince" is used in the same verse, apparently to refer to someone else, a bad guy who destroys the city and the sanctuary. If we go with this reading, one way to look at it would be that the decree to restore Jerusalem is actu- ally earlier than Cyrus, already proclaimed by Jeremiah himself (see Jer 30:18; 31:38–40) in anticipation of the end of exile. Then the decree to restore Jerusalem could be dated to 587 BC (when Jeremiah announced the decree), and seven weeks (49 years) later would take us to 538 BC, when Cyrus allowed the exiles to return home. In that case, maybe Cyrus himself is "the anointed prince" of Daniel 9:25. After all, Isaiah also calls Cyrus an anointed one (Isa 45:1). And then maybe the next anointed one, after another 62 weeks, the anointed one who is "cut off" in verse 26—maybe that could be the anointed high priest Onias III, who was killed by his enemies at the time of Antiochus IV Epiphanes in the second century BC. (The story of the ill-fated Onias III is told in 2 Maccabees 3–4.)[16] And then the last week of the 70 weeks

---

16. Something like this interpretation is argued in Joseph A. Fitzmyer, *The One*

might refer to the tribulation brought about by Antiochus himself, who is perhaps the prince who desolated the sanctuary. After all, we have already seen how interested the book of Daniel is in Antiochus IV (Dan 8), and we will see it again in our next chapter (when we talk about Dan 11). One more clue that the 70 weeks has something to do with Antiochus IV is the phrase "abomination of desolation" (Dan 9:27). That phrase is used again at Daniel 11:31, where it definitely has in view the period of Antiochus Epiphanes. That seems to be the meaning at Daniel 12:11, also. Of course, Jesus uses the same wording (Mark 13:14 // Matt 24:15) to talk about something the Romans would do in AD 70.

But the problem with this interpretation is the same one we've already seen with other interpretations: the calculation doesn't really work out, because there are simply not 434 years (62 weeks) between Cyrus (538 BC) and the murder of Onias III (171 BC). It's more like 368 years.

• Maybe we're not supposed to make these calculations.

Since that last suggestion is the one I lean toward, I'll develop it a little more now and again at the end of the chapter. No matter how we crunch the numbers or who we identify as the anointed prince, we're not going to come up with a simple and clear solution. Maybe the solution is not supposed to be clear and simple, but just the opposite. Maybe Gabriel wants to assure Daniel that God has everything worked out, but he also wants to prevent Daniel (and us!) from coming up with a calculation for when God is going to act. So Gabriel intentionally presents a confusing set of numbers and a vague set of references, to prevent us from crunching the numbers. God has it worked out so I don't need to. What I need to know is that God is going to take care of sin. I do not need to know when He is

---

Who Is to Come (Grand Rapids: Eerdmans, 2007), 61–63; and in the older commentary by S. R. Driver, *The Book of Daniel* (Cambridge: Cambridge University Press, 1900), 146; and in much modern biblical scholarship.

going to act, but I do need to know that God knows when He will act.

Verse 26

The different translations are best represented in chart-form.

KJV	NRSV
And after threescore and two weeks	After the sixty-two weeks
shall Messiah be cut off	an anointed one shall be cut off
but not for himself	and shall have nothing
and the people of the prince that shall come	and the troops of the prince who is to come
shall destroy the city and the sanctuary	shall destroy the city and the sanctuary
and the end thereof *shall be* with a flood	Its end shall come with a flood
and unto the end of the war desolations are determined	and to the end there shall be war. Desolations are decreed.

As we discussed with regard to verse 25, it is not clear here whether the anointed one (or the Messiah) who is cut off is supposed to be Jesus at His crucifixion, or maybe Onias III two centuries earlier, or something else. And the people that destroy the city and the sanctuary—are we talking about the Greeks at the time of Antiochus Epiphanes, or the Romans in AD 70, or something else?

What is clear is that some bad things are going to happen to God's people. This is included in God's plans.

Verse 27

The beginning of this verse is pretty much the same in all translations: "He shall make a strong covenant with many for one week, and for half of the week he shall make sacrifice and offering cease." But then the second part of the verse exhibits some difficulties that are interpreted in different ways.

KJV	NASB	NRSV
and for the overspreading of abominations he shall make *it* desolate, even until the consummation, and that determined shall be poured upon the desolate.	and on the wing of abominations will come one who makes desolate, even until a complete destruction, one that is decreed, is poured out on the one who makes desolate.	and in their place shall be an abomination that desolates, until the decreed end is poured out upon the desolator.

What in the world is this business about the first half of the seventieth week, and the second half? Maybe it would make sense as a reference to Antiochus Epiphanes, who made sacrifices and offerings cease for about 3 years or so. I guess it could possibly point to Jesus, whose sacrificial death on the cross nullified (in the minds of Christians) the sacrifices at the temple, and in that sense He made them cease, and this came after a ministry lasting about three years. Or maybe it refers to the Romans, who destroyed the temple and thus made sacrifices cease.[17] In any case, what do you do with the second half of the final week? A lot of Christian readers now and in ancient times took this last week as describing something that hasn't happened yet, something that an antichrist will do at the end of time. That view

---

17. For an argument that some first-century Jews read Daniel's seventy weeks as offering a chronological scheme soon to be fulfilled in their day, see Wright, *New Testament and the People of God*, 312–14 (where Wright interprets Josephus, *War* 6.312–15); idem, *Jesus and the Victory of God* (Minneapolis: Fortress, 1996), 349–53.

assumes that there's a gap between the first 69 weeks and the last week.[18]

Interpretations

This difficult passage has inspired many interpretations, which fact adds to the confusion rather than alleviating it.[19] As the early-twentieth-century scholar James A. Montgomery put it, "To sum up: The history of the exegesis of the 70 Weeks is the Dismal Swamp of O.T. criticism."[20] In the early fifth century, Jerome was already able to catalog ten different interpretations (nine Christian interpretations and a Jewish one). That number has surely increased over the sixteen centuries since Jerome's time. These days conservative Christians who want to interpret Daniel's seventy weeks argue about whether the "weeks of years" entail solar years (365 days) or lunar years (354 days) or prophetic years (supposedly 360 days) or jubilee periods.[21] Some inter-

---

18. For one presentation of this view, see J. Randall Price, "Prophetic Postponement in Daniel 9 and Other Texts," in *Issues in Dispensationalism*, ed. Wesley R. Willis and John R. Master (Chicago: Moody, 1994), 133–65. For a summary of a dispensational interpretation of Daniel 9:27 from a non-dispensationalist, see Brian P. Irwin and Tim Perry, *After Dispensationalism: Reading the Bible for the End of the World* (Bellingham, WA: Lexham, 2023), 74–81, 188–90.

19. For ancient Jewish interpretations, see Lester L. Grabbe, "The Seventy-Weeks Prophecy (Daniel 9:24–27) in Early Jewish Interpretation," in *The Quest for Context and Meaning: Studies in Biblical Intertextuality in Honor of James A. Sanders* (Leiden: Brill, 1997), 595–611; Roger T. Beckwith, "Daniel 9 and the Date of Messiah's Coming in Essene, Hellenistic, Pharisaic, Zealot and Early Christian Computation," *Revue de Qumran* 10 (1981): 521–42. There is not much explicit interpretation of the seventy weeks in pre-rabbinic Jewish sources, though there are hints in Josephus and the Dead Sea Scrolls and elsewhere that the prophecy inspired various thoughts and movements. For early Christian interpretations, see William Adler, "The Apocalyptic Survey of History Adapted by Christians: Daniel's Prophecy of 70 Weeks," in *The Jewish Apocalyptic Heritage in Early Christianity*, ed. James C. VanderKam and William Adler (Minneapolis: Fortress, 1996), 201–38.

20. James A. Montgomery, *The Book of Daniel*, International Critical Commentary (Edinburgh: T&T Clark, 1927), 400.

21. Instead of a "prophetic year," scholars of ancient calendars talk about a schematic year of 360 days; see Michael LeFebvre, *The Liturgy of Creation: Under-*

preters (dispensationalists) insert a gap between the 69th year and the 70th as if we are now (in the twenty-first century) living in the gap, anticipating the seventieth week.[22] A gap preceding the 70th week is an idea found already in one of the interpretations proposed by Eusebius, the well-known church historian in the fourth century.[23] Eusebius was not the first to propose a gap; this is an idea found also in the earliest commentary on Daniel, that of Hippolytus of Rome (second century AD).[24] There's nothing in Gabriel's message that would make one think that the 70th week does not follow immediately the 69th week, but—as we've seen—it's hard to get the dates to work in some other way.

This passage was recognized as difficult in early Christianity, so difficult that a single interpretation hardly did it justice. The aforementioned Eusebius forgoes offering a single interpretation and instead explores three different interpretations.[25] Here I summarize the main features of his three interpretations.

- Eusebius Interpretation 1: Eusebius names as his

---

standing Calendars in Old Testament Context (Downers Grove, IL: IVP, 2019), 99–103, with bibliography.

22. See the notes on this chapter in the Scofield Reference Bible (available online, e.g., at Wikisource), which explains in its comment on Daniel 9:24: "When the Church-age will end, and the seventieth week begin, is nowhere revealed. Its duration can be but seven years." For the dispensational account of the 70 weeks, see George M. Marsden, *Fundamentalism and American Culture*, 2d ed. (Oxford: Oxford University Press, 2006), 48–55; Glenn W. Shuck, "Christian Dispensationalism," in *The Oxford Handbook of Millennialism*, ed. Catherine Wessinger (Oxford: Oxford University Press, 2011), 515–28. For an account from a dispensationalist, see Ryrie, *Dispensationalism*. For a consideration and rejection of dispensationalism from a Christian confessional standpoint, see Irwin and Perry, *After Dispensationalism*. For a dispensationalist commentary on the entire book, see, e.g., John F. Walvoord, *Daniel: The Key to Prophetic Revelation* (Chicago: Moody, 1971).

23. Eusebius, *Demonstration of the Gospel* 8.2. For a translation, see Eusebius, *The Proof of the Gospel*, trans. W. J. Ferrar, 2 vols. (1920; repr. Grand Rapids: Baker, 1981), 2.131.

24. Hippolytus, *Commentary on Daniel* 4.35.3. For a translation, see T. C. Schmidt, *Hippolytus of Rome's Commentary on Daniel* (Piscataway, NJ: Gorgias, 2022), 168–69.

25. Eusebius goes through each of the three interpretations in his *Demonstration of the Gospel* 8.2.

source the earlier Christian writer Julius Africanus (third century), who insisted that one must use lunar years to get the calculation to work. The seventy years start in 444 BC (Neh 1–2) and come to an end with the death of Jesus Christ.

- Eusebius Interpretation 2: the anointed one of Daniel 9:25 is not Jesus Christ but rather the line of post-exilic high priests. The anointed one of verse 26 is Alexander Jannaeus in the early first century BC, whose death ("cut off," verse 26) marked the end of the independent kingdom of Judah under the Hasmoneans, sort of. Eusebius seems to locate the final fulfillment of the 490 years in Pompey's annexation of Judea in 63 BC.

- Eusebius Interpretation 3: from Darius the Great until the birth of Jesus. But even here Eusebius says that the anointed one that is cut off must be the high priest.[26]

It is not clear to Eusebius that the passage concerns the crucifixion of Jesus. That is one possibility among others. Perhaps the anointed one is a high priest, and maybe the prophecy is about the removal of the priesthood from the Jews. That is the line taken by Eusebius in his *Church History* (1.6.11), though he also points out that the removal of the Jewish priesthood aligns with the coming of Jesus Christ. That Daniel's seventy weeks find their fulfillment in Jesus has, however, been the usual Christian view. Origen did not offer a detailed exposition of our passage, but he did say that with the birth of Jesus "the seventy weeks until Christ the ruler, according to Daniel, were fulfilled" (*First Principles* 4.1.5).[27] But some saw the conclu-

---

26. For this point, see the translation of Ferrar, *Proof of the Gospel*, 131–32.

27. See Origen, *On First Principles: A Reader's Edition*, trans. John Behr (Oxford: Oxford University Press, 2019), 240. I have quoted Behr's translation of the preserved Greek text (printed on the lower portion of the page).

sion of the 490 years in Rome's destruction of Jerusalem in AD 70. This is the view taken by Tertullian (*Against the Jews* 8) and Clement of Alexandria (*Stromata* 1.21).[28]

My Take

I'll say it again: I don't know how to work out the details. The numerous proposals for interpretation surely indicate that no definitive interpretation can possibly be offered. I personally prefer to go with what I know—and when it comes to the Prophecy of the Seventy Weeks, what I know is that I don't understand it. Maybe God intended it that way? What if God sent Gabriel specifically to confuse Daniel—maybe "confuse" is the wrong word, since God is not the author of confusion (1 Cor 14:33), so how about "overwhelm," like He did to Job? God wanted to overwhelm Daniel, to unveil this complicated series of "weeks" in which all kinds of things would happen, but to unveil it in such a way that no one could possibly calculate when it would come to pass? At the same time, the prophecy offers assurance that God has a timetable in mind—it's just a timetable that He knows and we don't.

If that's the case, then God intended for the calculation to be hard, baffling, impossible. He did not intend for us to be able to figure out how to do the calculation. So there is no point in trying to figure out when to start counting. Is it at Cyrus' decree, or before that with Jeremiah's prophecy, or after that with Artaxerxes? The answer is, none of the above because we're not supposed to count. There is no need to get the numbers to work out. There is need only of praising God for taking care of our greatest problems on His own timetable. No one could have

---

28. This is also Jerome's view, apparently, as given in his *Chronicle*; see the edition of Rudolf Helm, *Eusebius Werke 7: Die Chronik des Hieronymus*, Die Griechischen Christlichen Schriftsteller der Ersten Jahrhunderte 47 (Leipzig: Hinrichs, 1913), 114. On this passage of the *Chronicle*, see Grabbe, "Seventy-Weeks Prophecy," 610.

taken this prophecy and worked out when the events described in it were going to take place. We know that for sure because over the millennia people have tried again and again and they've been proven wrong each time.

As scholar Michael Segal said about the seventy weeks,

> These numbers should be understood typologically and not as precise calculations. The typological nature of these numbers is the primary reason that interpreters have been unable to satisfactorily align them with the dates of actual historical events (including Dan 9). They were never intended to reflect a historical reality but rather an idealized, schematic view of history and its periodization.[29]

Similarly, commentator Carol Newsom draws this conclusion from the many interpretations on offer:

> The remarkably diverse set of suggestions that all require some adjustment to match the time line suggests that the author was not intending to make a precise chronological calculation but simply to connect important events in history by means of a symbolic heptadonal system of time.[30]

I think the main idea of Daniel's seventy weeks is that God has His own timetable for working things out. But there are also some other points we can derive from this passage.

- Things are not going to get better immediately.
- God is in control.
- Human rulers are not in control.
- God has a plan for bringing an end to sin.

---

29. Segal, "Chronological Conception," 294.
30. Newsom and Breed, *Daniel*, 303.

The expiation of Israel's sin will not take 70 years, the time period Jeremiah allotted for the exile, but rather 70 x 7. Again, this way of putting Daniel's seventy weeks reminds Christian readers of the statement from Jesus in Matthew 18:24, where Jesus gives a number interpreted literally by no one, least of all Jesus. Thank God that Jesus does not stop offering forgiveness once we've sinned against Him 490 times (or 77 times or whatever).

Conclusion

Daniel prays for God to remove the sin of His people, and Gabriel assures Daniel that God will do just that. When? Gabriel's complex calculus often leaves readers baffled, which may have been the point. Without a workable chronology to predict God's actions, Daniel was left with only one option: to trust God.

Discussion Questions

- What motivates Daniel's prayer in chapter 9?
  Compare Daniel 9:1–3 with Jeremiah 25:1–14; 29:1–14.
- What sort of prayer does Daniel pray? Why does he pray this prayer? What does he hope that God will do?
- What message does Gabriel bring to Daniel? Is this message supposed to bring Daniel comfort, or just information, or something else?
- What is supposed to happen during the seventy weeks that Gabriel mentions?
- Do you think there are one or two "anointed" ones in this prophecy? Are they—or is he—positive characters or negative ones?

Chapter 10
Angelic Rulers

I t was the apostle Paul who told the Christians in Ephesus that "we wrestle not against flesh and blood, but against principalities, against powers, against the rulers of the darkness of this world, against spiritual wickedness in high places" (Eph 6:12). Paul exhibited no interest in explaining what he meant by "spiritual wickedness in high places," only in telling Christians how to resist such spiritual wickedness by donning "the whole armor of God," including truth and righteousness and peace and faith and salvation and Scripture and prayer. But Paul's readers have not always shared the apostle's disinterest in detailing the evil spiritual forces opposed to God's people, and the chapter in Daniel we come to now has featured prominently in these discussions.

You will probably get tired of me saying this, but I insist that we know far less about the interpretation of Daniel than people often imagine. I think that statement applies to most chapters of this wonderful book, and it applies to Daniel 10. The statements about angels here are suggestive and have possible connections with other passages in Scripture—connections that we will explore here. We will do some dot-connecting in this chapter, but I think it is important for us to recognize that we—

not God—are the ones connecting the dots, and the resulting image might be off-base a little (or a lot). We will speculate on what Daniel 10 and other passages of Scripture might tell us about the spiritual forces at work in the world, but I prefer to follow Paul's lead in affirming without dwelling on spiritual warfare while directing Christians toward the habits and ideas that will guard their souls.

Overview

Though there are two chapters in Daniel after this one, we have arrived at the last vision of the book. The final three chapters of Daniel (chapters 10–12) constitute a single vision. Here is an overview of these chapters:

- Chapter 10: an angel visits Daniel
- Chapter 11: king-by-king look at battles between the Ptolemies and the Seleucids in the third and second centuries BC.
- Chapter 12: seal up the vision

Context

The date reference in this chapter assigns these events to the third year of King Cyrus of Persia, whose reign over Babylon began in about 539 BC. This is the only section of the book of Daniel that is dated to the reign of Cyrus.

Daniel had returned to his earlier diet of vegetables and water, because he had been mourning (10:2–3). He does not tell us what led to his mourning. Is he mourning over the sins of Israel? Has someone close to him died? He does not say. But later the "man" that visits Daniel says that Daniel had set his mind to gain understanding and to humble himself before his God (10:12). What did Daniel want to understand? The man says, I "have come to help you understand what is to happen to your people at the end of days" (10:14)—so I guess that's what Daniel wanted to know. I assume Daniel was thinking—okay, the exile is over, and it doesn't seem like things are really all that much better. What are God's plans?

The "man" says that he will reveal to Daniel "what is inscribed in the book of truth" (10:21). I guess that image represents the future as already written in a book, and Daniel is now going to be privileged with a sneak peek at that book.

Daniel says that he was located on the banks of the Tigris River, which means that he is not in the city of Babylon, which was on the Euphrates River. At Babylon, the two rivers are separated by about 60 miles. There are only two passages in the Hebrew Bible that mention the Tigris river by name, here and Genesis 2:14 in a description of the Garden of Eden. The Euphrates, in contrast, is mentioned a few dozen times in the Hebrew Bible (but never in the book of Daniel).

MAP 10.1: The Tigris and Euphrates Rivers (via Wikimedia Commons)[1]

Daniel sees in his vision a man with a distinctive appearance who has brought him a message. Daniel takes pains to clarify that "the people who were with me did not see the vision, though a great trembling fell upon them, and they fled and hid themselves" (10:7). This is not the only story in the Bible in which there is a strong spiritual presence in a certain location, but not all of the people in that location are equally aware of that spiritual presence—some are more attuned to it than others. We can cite the example of Balaam with his spiritually perceptive donkey (Num 22:22–30)—are animals always more spiritually perceptive than people? do dogs, for instance, sense unseen things better than humans do?—or Elisha, who asked God to open the eyes of his servant so that he could see that

---

1. https://commons.wikimedia.org/wiki/File:N-Mesopotamia_and_Syria_english.svg

"they that be with us are more than they that be with them" (2 Kgs 6:16–17), or that zealous Pharisee on his way to Damascus on a mission from the High Priest, who was suddenly blinded by a great light and heard a voice addressing him, while his companions only heard indistinctly a sound (Acts 9:7, 22:9). Daniel's companions could not see what Daniel saw, but they perceived that something was going on and they fled, leaving Daniel with the man that only he could see.

What Daniel sees is "a man clothed in linen" (10:5), whose appearance is described in some detail (10:5–6). For Christian readers, the description of this man in linen is reminiscent of the description of the son of man given in Revelation 1:12–16, a description of Jesus. In the case of the book of Daniel, the obvious guess is that this man in linen is an angel, and he may well be Gabriel, who has already visited Daniel a couple of times. The connection with Gabriel comes at Daniel 11:1, where this man in linen mentions "the first year of Darius the Mede," perhaps a reference to Daniel 9:1, which is a chapter involving Gabriel.[2]

The man in linen has come to help Daniel "understand what is to happen to your people at the end of days" (10:14). This revelation that the man in linen brings is the content of Daniel 11, which we'll get to in the next chapter. For now, we will consider not the message that the man in linen has come to tell Daniel, but rather what the man in linen says delayed his delivery of the message.

Angels over Nations?

Reflect on these two verses.

---

2. On the idea that readers are supposed to understand that the man in linen is Gabriel, see John J. Collins, *The Apocalyptic Imagination: An Introduction to Jewish Apocalyptic Literature*, 3d ed. (Grand Rapids: Eerdmans, 2016), 136.

But the prince of the kingdom of Persia (שַׂר מַלְכוּת פָּרַס, *sar malkut Paras*) opposed me twenty-one days. So Michael, one of the chief princes (הַשָּׂרִים הָרִאשֹׁנִים, *ha-sarim ha-rishonim*), came to help me, and I left him there with the prince of the kingdom of Persia[3] (Dan 10:13).

Then he said, "Do you know why I have come to you? Now I must return to fight against the prince of Persia, and when I am through with him, the prince of Greece will come" (Dan 10:20).

Who is the prince of the kingdom of Persia, and why is he in conflict with the man in linen? Probably most of my readers have an idea of what we're talking about, and I think you're probably right: we seem to be encountering a spiritual battle, or a battle among spirits, angelic warfare. As I've already mentioned, I am assuming that the "man in linen" is an angel, and I assume the same for the "prince of Persia." After all, what sort of "prince" could oppose an angel (the man in linen)? It must be an angelic prince. Moreover, Michael, also called a "prince" here (10:21), is a well-known angel, not only in Daniel, but also in the New Testament (Jude 9; Rev 12:7) and in Jewish literature[4]—and, of course, in Christian history; Michael's feast day, September 29, in the western tradition is known as Michaelmas. The word "prince" in Daniel 10 seems to apply not to a human ruler but to an angelic one. I should point out that "ruler" comes up several times in the New Testament (especially Paul's letters) as a label for

---

3. For "prince of the kingdom of Persia," the Old Greek has ὁ στρατηγὸς βασιλέως Περσῶν, "the captain of the king of the Persians," whereas Theodotion has ὁ ἄρχων βασιλείας Περσῶν, "the ruler of the kingdom of the Persians." Both Greek translations use ἄρχων in reference to Michael.

4. See, e.g., Darrell D. Hannah, *Michael and Christ: Michael Traditions and Angel Christology in Early Christianity* (Tübingen: Mohr Siebeck, 2009).

angels.[5] We have already seen the word in the quotation of Ephesians 6:12 at the top of this chapter.

So our "princes" or "rulers" are angels, but why are they connected with specific countries: "prince of Persia"; "prince of Greece"? Our "man in linen" describes Michael as "your prince" (10:21)—or, I should say, "y'all's prince," since the "you" here is plural. I take it, then, that Michael is the angelic ruler of Judah. Let me go ahead and present an interpretation, and then we'll look for evidence (biblical verses) for the interpretation. The idea in Daniel 10 may be that God set particular angels over particular nations, and maybe some of those angels rejected God's authority and misled the nations under their control, perhaps arranging for the people of that nation to worship the angel as a god. And maybe that has something to do with the conflict among the angels that the man in linen reports.

Now, what evidence could support this portrait of ruling angels? Well, there's Daniel 10. Do you need more? In the Old Testament, there are a few other passages worth mentioning, but they're not as explicit as Daniel 10. There are some relevant verses in the New Testament, and then there is Jewish tradition, contemporary with the New Testament and later.

First, let's review Daniel 10. Our angel—even if he is Gabriel —is apparently simply a messenger from God, perhaps a very important messenger, perhaps with a great deal of authority, but apparently not with authority over any particular nation. Michael is "y'all's prince" (10:21, cf. 12:1), apparently meaning that he is the prince over Israel (but how to jibe that with Deut 32:8–9?). Our messenger also mentions a prince of Persia (vv. 13, 20) and a prince of Greece (v. 20), and the prince of Greece will come after the prince of Persia. This is all being revealed during the days of Cyrus, king of Persia (10:1), so what we are to under-

---

5. A few times it's the very same Greek word that appears in Daniel 10, ἄρχων, *archōn* (Eph 2:2; cf. 1 Cor 2:6, 8). Other times, Paul uses the closely related word ἀρχαί, *archai* (Rom 8:38; Eph 3:10, 6:12; Col 1:16, 2:15).

stand is that conflicts in our world correspond to a spiritual struggle. Persia will be dominant in our world until "the prince of Greece" overtakes "the prince of Persia," at which point Greece will become the dominant power in our world. Readers of Daniel already know that Greece is going to follow Persia as a kingdom in our world because that was the point of the ram and goat in Daniel 8 (cf. 8:20–21). Maybe one aspect of this business of ruling angels suggested by Daniel 10 is that the conflicts among nations on earth mirror the conflicts among the ruling angels beyond human vision.

Why would the prince of Persia oppose this man in linen? Hmm. Maybe it's because the man in linen reports to Daniel about the defeat of Persia by Greece (11:2–3). I can imagine an objection to that suggestion: surely a decree from God about kingdoms would not be altered simply by stopping or delaying the report about that decree! I do not disagree with that reasoning, but maybe the "prince of Persia" thought that if he could just stop the delivery of the message, it would buy him some time to think of a plan to overcome the "prince of Greece." How's that work for you? Do you have a better suggestion for why the prince of Persia opposed the man in linen?

Jerome had a different interpretation: he thought that the opposition was not aimed at keeping Persia in power over against Greece but in keeping the Jews in captivity in Persian lands. "And so the prince or angel of the Persians offered resistance, acting on behalf of the province entrusted to him, in order that the entire captive nation might not be released." Jerome imagines that the form of the opposition was not military but "enumerating the sins of the Jewish people as a ground for their justly being kept in captivity and as proof that they ought not to be released." According to Jerome, the man in linen (perhaps Gabriel) was praying to God on behalf of Daniel, and he was joined by Michael, Israel's angel. Jerome asserted that the Greek angel was coming to argue against the Persian angel so that the Greeks might succeed the Persians. For Jerome, this spiritual battle was more spiritual than battle.

That's about as much speculating on Daniel 10 as I can do. There are a couple of other Old Testament passages to consider, as well. Prominent here is Deuteronomy 32:8, which says that YHWH "fixed the borders of the peoples according to the number of the sons of God" (ESV). Again, that verse is pretty obscure, but let's imagine for a moment that its meaning is that God divided up the nations ("the borders of the peoples") so that each nation could have its own angel ("sons of God"). If that is how to understand Deuteronomy 32:8, the meaning would be similar to a common understanding of Daniel 10. But I will acknowledge that the way the ESV reads at Deuteronomy 32:8 is not the way every translation reads; some have "sons of Israel" rather than "sons of God," so the interpretation I have suggested here is by no means definite.

I'll briefly mention one more passage from the Old Testament. Psalm 82 is again difficult to interpret, but it seems to represent YHWH bringing judgment against some other gods who had failed to promote justice on earth. This psalm could make sense as if YHWH condemns the national angels (the gods) of other nations for their malfeasance. If that's right, then we have another passage that depicts angels in charge of nations, some of whom were opposed to God, just as seems to be the case in Daniel 10.

Before getting to the New Testament, I'll point out that I am not simply making all this up. Some ancient Jewish literature outside the Hebrew Bible affirms these ideas. I'll give two examples, both from the second century BCE. First, from the deuterocanonical book of Sirach: "He appointed a ruler for every nation, but Israel is the Lord's own portion" (Sir 17:17). It seems like Sirach would be talking about angelic rulers for each nation since that situation is contrasted with Israel's relationship with the Lord. The second example comes from the pseudepigraphical book of Jubilees, which in one passage says that God "made spirits rule over all ... but over Israel he made no angel or spirit rule because he alone is their ruler" (Jub 15:31–32).[6] That seems pretty clear.

Now to the New Testament. No passage comes right out and says (in the manner of Jubilees) that angels rule nations—not anywhere close. But there are some passages that say or imply that the devil rules nations. Is that because the devil is a fallen angel? Well, the Bible never says that the devil is a fallen angel, but a lot of people throughout history have thought that the devil was a fallen angel, soooo ....

What are these passages that say that the devil rules nations? First off, Satan himself claims it when he's trying to tempt Jesus (Luke 4:8–9). Maybe Satan is lying (he does that kind of thing), but maybe he's not. Maybe he really does have control over the kingdoms of the world. Elsewhere Jesus seems to be referring to Satan when He talks about "the ruler (*archōn*) of this world" (John 12:31, 14:30, 16:11), and a common interpretation of Paul's phrase "the god of this world" (2 Cor 4:4) is that it refers to Satan.[7] You might also want to consult Revelation 13, which depicts the Satanic dragon as calling forth the beast from the sea, a representation of the Roman Empire.

Conclusion

We have spent more time dwelling on this theme than the Bible does anywhere in its pages. I think it is important to note that the Bible tells us that there are things going on behind the scenes, things hidden from our view, but it's not really interested in giving us more than a quick peek, and that only rarely. In other words, the Bible does not encourage readers to spend time

---

6. Translation in James C. VanderKam, *Jubilees*, 2 vols., Hermeneia (Minneapolis: Fortress, 2018), 1.507. On the interpretation of this passage, see Vander-Kam, 1.521–24; Ryan E. Stokes, *The Satan: How God's Executioner Became the Enemy* (Grand Rapids: Eerdmans, 2019), 87, 94–98.

7. See Derek R. Brown, *The God of This Age* (Tübingen: Mohr Siebeck, 2015).

thinking about spiritual forces other than God. God is in control; no other force—natural or supernatural—can compare to Him, and the book of Daniel could serve as Exhibit A for that claim. Remember when Jesus said that we should only fear the one who can throw both soul and body in hell (Matt 10:28)? Only God has such power.

With that major caveat in place, we have spent so much time thinking about the spiritual forces in the world because the Bible does contain these hints. There have been a lot of guesses over the years about what these hints are pointing to, and it could be helpful to us to see what sort of evidence there is for these views. The answer: some, not much.

Daniel 10 does show us that one of these "princes" slowed down the "man in linen," thereby delaying the delivery of his message. The prince did not stop the delivery of the message, but it did slow him down. That is some amount of power on the part of the prince, to delay a divine messenger. I have two thoughts about this episode. First, and to echo Jesus, this prince would have no power over one of God's messengers if it were not given him from above (cf. John 19:11)—and I mean that literally. The prince has only so much power as God allows, and the prince could not possibly delay an angel from God without God's approval. I love how *Paradise Lost* describes the primordial battle in heaven between Satan's angels and God's angels (book 6). The battle was pretty much evenly split until the Son of God decided to get involved, and at that point, Satan's forces were immediately cast out of heaven. That seems about right. The buck stops with God.

Second, I am reminded of Paul's statement in 1 Thessalonians 2:18 that Paul had been wanting to visit the Thessalonians "but Satan blocked our way." That is one way to look at it. No doubt, Satan would like to have blocked Paul from going everywhere to spread the gospel. Paul wrote to the Thessalonians from Corinth, a ministry described in Acts 18. Paul did a lot of good while Satan was keeping him out of Thessalonica. In another passage, Paul was trying to evangelize in parts of Asia but he was being prevented—this time, not by Satan but by the Spirit of God (Acts 16:6–7). The Spirit had other plans, specifically, sending Paul and Silas into Europe (16:10). I assume Satan was rather happy that Paul had been unable to preach in all the locations of Asia that he wanted. But in the end, the kingdom of Satan took a hit because the Spirit was directing Paul elsewhere.

What I'm getting at is that Satan blocked Paul's way to Thessalonica, but that move wasn't necessarily a net win for Satan. It really depends on what Paul was willing to do in the places that God allowed him to work. Did he sit and grumble about not being about to get to Thessalonica? Did he decide to binge the new season of *Cobra Kai*? We happen to know that since Paul was stuck in Corinth, he decided to work for the Lord in Corinth. You might remember the same sort of thing happening in Athens (Acts 17:16–34). The Apostle bloomed where he was planted; he worked where and when God allowed him to work. Satan was involved, sure, but he wasn't calling the shots.

The man in linen was delayed in his approach to Daniel. No great loss to the cause of God or to Daniel himself if Daniel spent the intervening time doing God's work where he was.

The lesson: yes, evil spirits exist and have some power. They can do what God allows them to do. They may be able to prevent us from doing some things we want to do, but they cannot prevent us from serving the Lord, even if they force us to be creative about how we are serving the Lord.

Discussion Questions

- In this chapter, Daniel encounters a man dressed in linen. Who do you think this person is?
- The man in linen tells Daniel about the prince of Persia and the prince of Greece, and about Michael.

Who is Michael, and what is his role? Who are the princes that are mentioned?

- Are the princes in a conflict? What is causing the conflict?
- How important do you think it is for Christians to recognize the influence of evil spiritual forces in life?
- What is the relationship of these evil spiritual forces to our God?

Chapter 11
Caught in the Middle

Have you ever noticed that the wrong sort of people tend to be in charge of government? I don't mean the civil servants but the leaders at the top. Generally speaking, humans throughout the world and throughout time have suffered under leaders who seek their own interests before the interests of others. I will say that I think such leaders attain power in modern democracies proportionately less often than in other systems of government, but no one could claim that the American system of government, for instance, is immune to such leaders. Is that the fault of the people who attain those positions of power or a fault of the position itself? Is it that the people who attain those positions of power are just bad people, or that the position has a damaging influence on their souls? I think it's probably a combination. We should not underestimate how bad it can be for you to have the authority to tell others what to do. I am reminded of this statement from Barton Stone in 1843:

> I never yet have seen the man, elected to Congress, or to a State Legislature, that returned home a better man, more religiously disposed and religiously engaged. On the contrary, if they had

been religious before, they returned less so, barren and dead to God, and divine things.[1]

That analysis suggests that the job itself may be bad for your spiritual well-being. I think there's some truth to that. We know that power corrupts. But it could also be true that the people who desire such power and are willing to do what it takes to attain such power are not the best people.

And the people of God are often caught in the middle, suffering for the arrogance and ambition of others. That is the message brought to Daniel by the man in linen, whom we met in Daniel 10. Now in Daniel 11, he reveals an alarming portrait of the future, but he also assures Daniel that God has matters in hand.

The Ptolemies and the Seleucids

The message that the man in linen brought to Daniel is a long narrative about the events transpiring in Egypt and the Levant during the late fourth century BC through the mid-second century BC. At the very beginning of the chapter, we get a reference to Alexander the Great (the "mighty king" of verse 3) and his overthrow of the Persian Empire. Most of the chapter concerns the Greek kings that fought over Alexander's empire upon the death of this mighty king in 323 BC—the Greek kings and the dynasties they established. Actually, Daniel 11 is concerned with only two dynasties, both named for the first king that ruled the dynasty: the Ptolemies in Egypt and the Seleucids in Asia (especially Mesopotamia and Syria). The reason it is these two dynasties that serve as the focus of attention is because, during the period between Alexander and the coming

---

1. Barton W. Stone, "Reflections of Old Age," *Christian Messenger* (August 1843): 123–26, at 123. See further D. Newell Williams, *Barton Stone: A Spiritual Biography* (St. Louis: Chalice, 2000), ch. 19.

of the Romans in 63 BC, these were the two great powers that dictated affairs in Judah. Judah was caught in the middle between them.

The Ptolemies and the Seleucids are not named in Daniel 11. Rather, the Ptolemies are called the kings of the south and the Seleucids are called the kings of the north. If you read a history book about this time period, it will be pretty easy to see which verse of Daniel 11 corresponds to which Ptolemaic or Seleucid king.

Like the vision in Daniel 8, this revelation builds up to "a contemptible person" (11:21) who becomes the Seleucid king. This is Antiochus IV Epiphanes (reigned 175–164 BC), remembered in Jewish tradition as an infamous persecutor of Jews who provoked the Maccabean rebellion, recorded in the apocryphal books of Maccabees and commemorated annually at the festival of Hanukkah. As the boastful little horn on the goat becomes the main focus of Daniel 8, so the revelation of Daniel 11 spends more time on this contemptible person than on any other king.

But Daniel 11 is not focused exclusively on Antiochus Epiphanes. The material that clearly corresponds to the life of Antiochus IV occupies verses 21–39 (or maybe 21–35). So before getting to him, there are twenty verses relating to the vicissitudes of the Hellenistic world. And the final six (or maybe ten) verses of the chapter, which seem to continue the account of Antiochus Epiphanes, do not correspond to what other sources tell us about his death, and so some interpreters have tried to relate them to other, later kings, perhaps a Roman ruler, perhaps the Antichrist.

The Details of Daniel 11

The Ptolemies and Seleucids were constantly fighting, and this ongoing conflict serves as one of the themes of Daniel 11. Traditionally, the wars between the Ptolemies and Seleucids have been labeled the Syrian Wars, of which there was a series in the third and second centuries BC. One could say that it was just one long war; perhaps we could call it the Hundred Years War if only that name were not already taken. But historians usually divide the long contest between these two kingdoms into different wars, and so they talk about the First Syrian War and the Second Syrian War, etc. Exactly when each war ended and another began is not clear and engenders some disagreement among modern scholars. One common way to divide the conflict is into six Syrian Wars.[2] That schema results in the following dates for the six wars.

1. 274–271 BC
2. 260–253 BC.
3. 246–251 BC = the Laodicean War
4. 219–217 BC
5. 202–198 BC. This war, won by Antiochus III the Great over Ptolemy V Epiphanes, witnessed the overlordship of Judah transferred from the Ptolemies to the Seleucids, at the Battle of Panium in 200 BC (see Josephus, *Antiquities of the Jews* 12.132).
6. 170–168 BC

The wars had a lot to do with the land of Judah, or actually the land called at the time Coelê Syria, somewhat broader than merely Judah.[3] Ptolemy had captured Coelê Syria early on, already in 320 BC, so he considered the territory his own.[4] But at a crucial battle among the other successors to Alexander, the Battle of Ipsus (301 BC), Ptolemy decided to stay home and not

---

2. See John D. Grainger, *The Syrian Wars* (Leiden: Brill, 2010), who counts nine of these wars.

3. See Lester L. Grabbe, *A History of the Jews and Judaism in the Second Temple Period*, 4 vols. (London: T&T Clark, 2004–2021), 2.173–76; Anca Dan and Étienne Nodet, *Cœlé-Syrie: Palestine, Judée* (Leuven: Peeters, 2017).

4. See Diodorus 18.43; Pat Wheatley, "Ptolemy Soter's Annexation of Syria, 320 BC," *Classical Quarterly* 45 (1995): 433–40.

get involved, so at the conclusion of this battle all of Syria was awarded to Seleucus. Ptolemy disputed the validity of that gift, and he maintained control of Coelê Syria, whereas Seleucus decided not to press the point immediately.[5] The matter would not remain dormant, especially after the death of the first generation of Hellenistic rulers. Appian (*Syr.* 52) explained why Coelê Syria was valuable: Ptolemy I wanted to control the region "because it was well situated for defending Egypt and for attacking Cyprus."

The first half of Daniel 11 concerns the Ptolemaic kings (= the king of the South) and the Seleucids kings (= the king of the North) up until the time of that boastful little horn (cf. Dan 8:9), Antiochus IV Epiphanes, who dominates the last half of the chapter (from verse 21).

The Hellenistic kings in play here are detailed below.[6] Verses 3–4 refer to Alexander the Great, king of Macedon, who died in Babylon just prior to turning 33 and left no obvious successor. Various Macedonian officials then vied for power, and the kingdom Alexander had conquered split up among various people, with the two most important ones for our purposes being Ptolemy and Seleucus. The former quickly established himself in Egypt and started a dynasty in which all of the male monarchs took Ptolemy's name. Seleucus, after serving for some time in Ptolemy's court, managed to gain control of "Syria" (including Mesopotamia) and established a dynasty in which the

---

5. See Diodorus 21.1.5; Victor Tcherikover, *Hellenistic Civilization and the Jews* (Philadelphia: JPS, 1959), 53; Susan Sherwin-White and Amélie Kuhrt, *From Samarkhand to Sardis: A New Approach to the Seleucid Empire* (Berkeley: University of California Press, 1993), 14.

6. For modern accounts of these two kingdoms, see J. G. Manning, *The Last Pharaohs: Egypt under the Ptolemies, 305–30 BC* (Princeton: Princeton University Press, 2012); and on the Seleucids, see Sherwin-White and Kuhrt, *From Samarkhand to Sardis*. On the matter of royal incest among the Hellenistic dynasties, see Sheila L. Ager, "Familiarity Breeds: Incest and the Ptolemaic Dynasty," *Journal of Hellenic Studies* 125 (2005): 1–34.

kings alternated between the name Seleucus and the name Antiochus.

verse	kings
5	king of the south = Ptolemy I Soter (died 282 BC) one of his officers = Seleucus I Nicator (died 281 BC)
6	king of the south = Ptolemy II Philadelphus (reigned 285–246 BC) king of the north = Antiochus II Theos (reigned 261–246 BC) daughter of the king of the south = Berenice
7–9	branch from her roots = Ptolemy III Euergetes (reigned 245–221 BC), brother of Berenice king of the north = Seleucus II Callinicus (reigned 246–225 BC)
10	his sons = sons of Seleucus II = Seleucus III Ceraunus (reigned 225–223 BC) and Antiochus III the Great (reigned 223–187 BC)
11–12	king of the south = Ptolemy IV Philopator (reigned 221–203 BC) king of the north = Antiochus III the Great
13–16	king of the north = Antiochus III the Great king of the south = Ptolemy V Epiphanes (of Rosetta Stone fame; reigned 203–181 BC)
17	a woman in marriage = Cleopatra I Syra, daughter of Antiochus III, given to Ptolemy V (193 BC)
18–19	death of Antiochus III
20	Seleucus IV Philopator (reigned 187–175 BC), son of Antiochus III
21–35 (or 39)	Antiochus IV Epiphanes (reigned 175–164 BC)
40 (or 36)–46	Antiochus? a Roman king/general? Antichrist?

WHY ALL THIS detail about events in the third and second century BC? Well, I don't think the man in linen brought this revelation to Daniel because he needed to know about the various marriage alliances between the Ptolemies and Seleucids, or the wars that they fought to break those alliances. The point is not so much in the trees but in the forest, but of course, you need trees to construct the forest. But when we try to step back and see the forest in Daniel 11, what image appears?

First, human rulers fight with one another, make alliances, and then fight some more. Shall we say this chapter illustrates the ephemeral nature of politics or governments? That has been a theme of the book of Daniel. Daniel himself is engaged in politics—maybe not at the time he receives his visit from the man in linen, but he has been involved in human government at the highest level. He knows better than most the wisdom of the Psalmist's counsel to "put not your trust in princes" (Ps 146:3). The endless—and ultimately fruitless—jockeying for position that we see in Daniel 11 reminds us again of this truth. I'll leave it to you to consider whether believers have yet learned this lesson.

Second, this chapter says something about the suffering endured by the people of God. Again, this theme is recurrent in the book of Daniel, most obvious in the experiences of the heroes of the book, who were variously thrown to the fire and to the lions. The apocalyptic visions in the second half of the book have also emphasized the coming tribulation on God's people. In Daniel 11, we see this motif, especially in relation to the section of the chapter that corresponds to the reign of Antiochus Epiphanes. Once he faces the Kittim in verse 30—that is, the Romans—he sates his wrath on the people of Judah. And so we read that "The wise among the people shall give understanding to many; for some days, however, they shall fall by sword and flame, and suffer captivity and plunder" (11:33). It's not the wicked among the people who suffer these things, but the wise. Their suffering is not deserved—quite the opposite. It is because they are "wise" that they suffer at the hands of those who despise such wisdom. Is there any need to remind my readers that such a perspective on suffering makes a frequent appearance in the New Testament and allows us to follow the path of our Lord, who told us to take up our own cross (Mark 8:34). Indeed, Jesus tells His followers to rejoice at such suffering (Matt 5:10–12), and Paul declares it a mark of God's grace (Phil 1:29). I have argued that the book of Daniel is a book against conformity to the world, and there is no greater mark of rejecting such conformity than in privileging God's wisdom over our comfort and even our physical safety.

This perspective on suffering leads naturally to a third point from Daniel 11. God is in control and He loves His people, despite what may be taken as evidence to the contrary. The suffering of God's people is no sign of divine impotence or callousness. As we see in this chapter, and in other chapters of Daniel, the suffering is temporary; as we will see in the next chapter, even the death of God's saints does not prevent Him from rewarding their righteousness.

The End of the Chapter

But what is going on at the end of the chapter? Starting in verse 21, the king of the north is pretty clearly Antiochus Epiphanes and one who knows the history of Antiochus can see a description of his career until a few verses from the end. But the death of the king of the north is related in verses 40–45, and this death does not correspond to what our other ancient sources— including Jewish sources—tell us about the death of Antiochus Epiphanes. Daniel describes the death of the king of the north in the final verse of the chapter: "He shall pitch his palatial tents between the sea and the beautiful holy mountain. Yet he shall come to his end, with no one to help him" (11:45). It sounds like he dies in Judah. While the ancient sources that we have on the death of Antiochus Epiphanes do not agree in every detail, they

all agree that Antiochus died in Persia or Babylon as a conse-
quence of trying to rob a pagan temple somewhere on that side
of his empire.[7] The entire last paragraph of Daniel 11, verses 40–
45, does not agree well with our other ancient sources for Antiochus Epiphanes, and some interpreters (especially traditional
ones) push back this lack of agreement all the way to verse 36,
which begins a description of how the king of the north disre-
garded the gods of his ancestors.[8]

What do we do with the last ten verses of this chapter? We
could say that our other sources are wrong and only Daniel 11
accurately describes the death of Antiochus Epiphanes, but most
readers have not been willing to take this position.[9] We could,
instead, say that Daniel 11 is wrong, that it intended to describe
the death of Antiochus Epiphanes but failed to do a good job.[10]
This suggestion has, understandably, not proven convincing to
most Christian readers. Some readers try to relate the details of

7. These sources include Polybius, *Histories* 31.9; Josephus, *Antiquities of the Jews*
12.354–59; 1 Maccabees 6:1–17; 2 Maccabees 1:13–16; 9:1–28. For a modern account
of the end of Antiochus IV, see John D. Grainger, *The Fall of the Seleukid Empire,
187–75 BC* (Barnsley: Pen & Sword, 2015), 35–38.
8. Critical scholars tend to see verse 40 as the break between material corre-
sponding to the known career of Antiochus Epiphanes and its opposite; see, e.g.,
James A. Montgomery, *The Book of Daniel*, International Critical Commentary
(Edinburgh: T&T Clark, 1927), 464–65; John E. Goldingay, *Daniel*, Word Biblical
Commentary (Dallas: Word, 1989), 305; John J. Collins, *Daniel: A Commentary on
the Book of Daniel*, Hermeneia (Minneapolis: Fortress, 1993), 388; Carol A.
Newsom and Brennan W. Breed, *Daniel: A Commentary*, Old Testament Library
(Louisville: WJK, 2014), 356–59. Interpreters who see in Daniel 11 a description
of the Antichrist tend to see the break at verse 36; see, e.g., J. Paul Tanner, *Daniel*,
Evangelical Exegetical Commentary (Bellingham, WA: Lexham, 2020), 685–706;
Wendy Widder, *Daniel*, Exegetical Commentary on the Old Testament (Grand
Rapids: Zondervan, 2023), 528.
9. But see Edward P. Myers, Neale T. Pryor, and David R. Rechtin, *Daniel*, Truth
for Today (Searcy, AR: Resource, 2012), 386–94, who do not actually contrast
Daniel with other ancient sources but try to harmonize the accounts such that
Daniel does truly speak of Antiochus Epiphanes at the end of Daniel 11. For
instance, they deny that Daniel 11:45 says that the king of the north will die in
Judah.
10. This is often the approach of critical scholars; see earlier citations of Montgomery, Collins, and Newsom.

Daniel 11:36–45 to some later king of the north, perhaps some Roman ruler.[11]

But the most popular Christian approach to the passage is to say that it relates to the end times, that here at the end of Daniel 11, we have a description of some evil ruler who will arise in the future and cause a great deal of trouble for God's people. In short, this approach sees at the end of Daniel 11 a description of the Antichrist.[12] People who read the text in this way tend to see the transition between Antiochus in verse 35 and the Antichrist in verse 36 as not totally abrupt since Antiochus himself is a forerunner or type of the Antichrist. In the words of George Eldon Ladd, "in verse 36 there appears to be a change in subject that looks beyond Antiochus to the Antichrist himself, of whom Antiochus was a type."[13] This is already the view of Jerome in the early fifth century AD, and, as he notes, he did not invent it.[14] Indeed, according to Ladd, it was Daniel who invented the concept of the Antichrist: "The idea of Antichrist first appears clearly in the Bible in the book of Daniel."[15] To which I would reply: I'm not sure how clearly it appears even here.

Look, I'm sure that some of my readers find the Antichrist interpretation of Daniel 11:36–45 to be deeply problematic and unconvincing. I agree. Some of my readers would want to push back on the entire concept of an Antichrist since this word appears in the Bible only a handful of times (1 John 2:18, 22; 4:3; 2 John 7) and never in reference to an end-time figure. Does the Bible reveal that immediately before the second advent of our

---

11. Robert M. Gurney, *God in Control: An Exposition of the Prophecies of Daniel* (West Sussex: H. E. Walter, 1980), 146–55; Jim McGuiggan, *The Book of Daniel* (Lubbock, TX: Montex, 1978), 226–36.

12. In addition to the commentaries mentioned earlier, this is also the view (surprisingly, to my mind) of James Burton Coffman, *Commentary on Daniel* (Abilene, TX: ACU Press, 1989), 174–77.

13. George Eldon Ladd, *The Last Things: An Eschatology for Laymen* (Grand Rapids: Eerdmans, 1978), 59.

14. Jerome, *Commentary on Daniel* 11:24.

15. Ladd, *Last Things*, 58.

Lord there will be a particularly heinous political ruler who will oppose God and his people? On the one hand, I could believe that it will happen; but on the other hand, does the Bible teach it? Hmm, I don't see it, not in any clear way—this figure of the Antichrist taught in the Bible, even without that name. I mean, I do see the man of sin in 2 Thessalonians 2, but I find the interpretation of that passage difficult. And I do know that the idea of an Antichrist goes back a long way, that already Christians in the second century AD had a pretty clearly defined idea of what they thought an Antichrist figure would look like.[16] The concept of the Antichrist at the end of time is clearly taught in Christian literature from the second century on,[17] but put me in the camp of those who don't see it clearly taught in Scripture.

Having said that, I acknowledge that the interpretation of Daniel 11:36–45 is difficult and uncertain. If the passage does not refer to Antiochus Epiphanes, and it doesn't refer to an endtimes Antichrist, I don't know what it does refer to. In that case, what we are left with is either admitting our ignorance or trying to press the details of the passage onto some other ancient king or onto Antiochus himself, which also seems a deeply unsatisfying interpretation.

Let me approach the Antichrist from another angle. First, the Bible may not clearly teach such a concept, but neither does

---

16. On the history of this idea, see Bernard McGinn, *Antichrist: Two Thousand Years of the Human Fascination with Evil* (San Francisco: HarperSanFrancisco, 1994); Robert Fuller, *Naming the Antichrist: The History of an American Obsession* (Oxford: Oxford University Press, 1995); Philip C. Almond, *The Antichrist: A New Biography* (Cambridge: Cambridge University Press, 2020); Mateusz Kusio, *The Antichrist Tradition in Antiquity: Antimessianism in Second Temple and Early Christian Literature* (Tübingen: Mohr Siebeck, 2020).

17. See, e.g., Hippolytus, *On Christ and Antichrist*. In the last quarter of the second century AD, Irenaeus of Lyon wrote about the Antichrist in such a way in his *Against Heresies* that Almond, *Antichrist*, 18, feels justified in declaring, "With Irenaeus ... the legend of the Antichrist begins." It was in the tenth century that a biography of the Antichrist was first written by Adso of Montier-en-Der, *Letter on the Origin and Time of the Antichrist*; for an English translation, see Bernard McGinn, trans., *Apocalyptic Spirituality* (New York: Paulist, 1979), 81–96.

it deny the concept. Maybe there will be an Antichrist at the end of time; the Bible doesn't really say, as far as I can tell. But let me ask you this: Is it true that there are always going to be political leaders who arrogate to themselves the privileges properly accorded only to the divine? And will these political leaders cause harm to the righteous? Yes, I think that is true. The past century of world history has seen its share of such leaders. You can probably think of such political leaders in power at this very moment. Will there be such political leaders until the end of the age? Will there be such political leaders at the end of the age? If I were a betting man, I'd put money on that. Will there be one such political leader at the end of the age who is especially nefarious? Such is the long-standing Christian tradition, and even without direct revelation on the point, I would not be shocked if at the end of time, there is a very prominent and nefarious political leader who is opposed to God and His messiah, who is anti-God and anti-Christ.

Can such a lesson be derived from Daniel 11? In my mind, only in a very general way. This chapter does show us a series of callous and harmful political leaders with power over God's people, leading to an especially callous and harmful political leader, Antiochus Epiphanes, and then a description of a political leader that is even more callous and harmful and whose death is narrated, but whose identity is debated. Perhaps we are to understand that such political leaders do come routinely and will continue to come until God puts down all rule and authority in opposition to Him. Though the people of God are often caught in the middle, we are assured of being caught in God's protection and mercy.

Can It Be About Antiochus Epiphanes?

A straightforward reading of Daniel 11 certainly gives the impression that we are talking about the same guy from verse 21 to verse 45. When there is a change from one "king of the north/south" to another in Daniel 11, the transition is some-times made explicit. Not always—the transition is somewhat invisible when we move from verse 5 (Ptolemy I and Seleucus I) to verse 6 (Ptolemy II and Antiochus II). But notice verse 7: "a branch from her roots shall rise up in his place," clearly marking the transition from Ptolemy II to Ptolemy III. Or verse 10, which mentions "his sons," that is, the sons of Seleucus II (i.e., Seleucus III and Antiochus III), who now become the focus for several verses. When Antiochus III dies in verse 19, we learn that a new king (Seleucus IV) "shall arise in his place" (v. 20). And when Seleucus IV dies as soon as he is introduced, the prophecy reveals that "in his place shall arise a contemptible person" (v. 21), obviously Antiochus Epiphanes. So, it is not unreasonable to expect some sort of a marker indi-cating a transition away from Antiochus Epiphanes in verse 36 or verse 40, if the prophecy has truly turned its attention to some other ruler. All that to say, it seems like this entire passage, verses 21–45, is most reasonably read as concerning Antiochus Epiphanes.

If the passage is about Antiochus Epiphanes, it is either right or wrong. Some modern scholars have read the passage as if it is an inaccurate depiction of the death of Antiochus; the predic-tion proved wrong. But if that is the case, why is it preserved at all? No doubt many false prophecies were spoken in ancient Israel, but we barely have any reference to them preserved in some scattered passages in our Bible (see, e.g., Deut 13:1–5; 1 Kings 22; Jer 23:9–22, 28). Why weren't false prophecies preserved? Because they were false. Remember what Moses told the Israelites about how to tell a prophecy of YHWH from a fake: "When a prophet speaketh in the name of the LORD, if the thing follow not, nor come to pass, that *is* the thing which the LORD hath not spoken, *but* the prophet hath spoken it presumptuously: thou shalt not be afraid of him" (Deut 18:22). If the prophecy did not come to pass, the prophet that spoke it is not YHWH's spokesman. But the ancient Jews considered

Daniel an authentic spokesman from YHWH, so they must
have thought that his prophecies proved accurate.

Let me come at this another way. There are disagreements
about when exactly the prophecy of Daniel 11 was written, with a
traditional view pitted against a modern scholarly view. Most
modern scholars think this prophecy was written during the lifetime of Antiochus Epiphanes. But everyone—traditionalist and
critical scholars alike—agrees that this prophecy was written
before the death of Antiochus Epiphanes. And everyone agrees
that very soon after his death, this prophecy was received by
Jews as holy Scripture. When ancient Jews experienced the
torments of Antiochus Epiphanes and then learned about his
sudden death, apparently they read this prophecy as revealing
divine truth about a frightful tyrant cut down in his arrogance.

But it is generally agreed that the details do not correspond
very closely to Antiochus Epiphanes.[18] Does that mean the
prophecy is not about him? Could it be about an Antichrist, as
most Christians throughout the ages have believed? It seems to
me that the only reason to read the last six or ten verses as
concerning the Antichrist is because some of the details in the
prophecy seem not to fit with what we otherwise know about
Antiochus Epiphanes.[19] Anyone privileged to encounter this
prophecy before the death of Antiochus would not have had
such a reason to seek an interpretation not involving him. In
other words, only after the death of Antiochus might someone
have seen here a prophecy of the Antichrist—in an attempt to
redeem an apparent false prophecy that failed to accurately
predict the details about the death of Antiochus. But is that how

---

18. A point denied by Myers, Pryor, and Rechtin, *Daniel*, 386–94.
19. A caveat: Jerome took the entire second half of the chapter to refer to the
Antichrist rather than Antiochus, even though he recognized that some of the
details easily fit the career of Antiochus. However, he also pointed out details in
this chapter that did not fit Antiochus, so he still might have been motivated to
see the Antichrist here because of the apparent lack of coherence with
Antiochus.

Jews in the second century BC who heard about the death of
Antiochus interpreted the prophecy? We have no evidence to
suggest that anyone interpreted this prophecy in terms of an
Antichrist until Christian times, nor do we have evidence that a
group of Jews in antiquity wondered whether Daniel was a false
prophecy—whereas we do have evidence of Jews wondering
about the inspiration or acceptability of Ezekiel, for instance, or
Esther, or Ecclesiastes.[20] But not Daniel. On the contrary,
almost immediately after Antiochus' death seems to have
demonstrated that the book contained inaccurate predictions,
we have evidence (from Qumran and the Greek translations)
that Jews highly valued the book and considered it Scripture.

The upshot of all this discussion is that the Jews who
suffered under Antiochus Epiphanes presumably regarded the
last ten verses of the chapter to depict truthfully the demise of
this brutal tyrant. How can that be, if the details don't match?

Let's think about Israelite prophecy and its fulfillment—or
even other prophecies in the book of Daniel. I have heard in
church all my life that Daniel 2 is fulfilled in Acts 2, that the
sermon by Peter and the invitation to respond to the gospel in
Acts 2 is the moment when God established his kingdom, in
fulfillment of Daniel 2:44 ("the God of heaven will set up a
kingdom that shall never be destroyed"). But the details of Acts
2 do not correspond very closely to the details of Daniel 2. If
Acts 2 represents a fulfillment of Daniel 2—a point I heartily
concede—we learn not to press the details of the prophecy. The
same is true for many messianic prophecies in the Hebrew Bible,
which only loosely correspond to their fulfillments in the New
Testament. In other words, I haven't seen any wolves and lambs
lying down together (cf. Isa 11:6). John Goldingay, in his
commentary on Daniel, makes this same point about messianic

20. On ancient Jewish questions regarding the status of these books, see Edmon
L. Gallagher and John D. Meade, *The Biblical Canon Lists from Early Christianity:
Texts and Analysis* (Oxford: Oxford University Press, 2017), 261–84.

prophecy and then gives the general rule: "It is not the nature of biblical prophecy to give a literal account of events before they take place."[21]

When prophecies in the Bible do not come to pass, there are several ways we might understand what God intends—or, to put it another way, why such unfulfilled prophecies have been preserved in our Scriptures. Perhaps God changed His mind, as in the case of Jonah's threat of destruction against Nineveh. Perhaps the promised outcome failed to materialize for some other reason, a point on which God reflects in His communication with Ezekiel regarding the failure of Nebuchadnezzar to receive payment in his siege of the city of Tyre (Ezek 29:17–20). Perhaps, from our vantage point, the prophecy awaits ultimate fulfillment, even if elements of the prophecy have already appeared; this is the "already/not yet" scenario. Perhaps the prophecy is fulfilled in a symbolic way. I'm not sure that "symbolic" is the right word here, but I think it communicates what I intend to say.

Think for a moment about the Old Testament prophecies about the blessed future that awaits God's people—prophecies such as the raising up of the mountain of the house of YHWH in Isaiah 2 and Micah 4, or the new heavens and new earth in Isaiah 65, or the temple vision of Ezekiel, or the promise at the end of Amos that "the one who plows shall overtake the one who reaps" (Amos 9:13). Would the New Testament authors say that such prophecies find fulfillment in the here and now via a spiritual interpretation in reference to the church? Or would they say that Christians will experience such bliss in the hereafter? Dispensationalists insist that these prophecies will be fulfilled literally in reference to Israel during the millennial reign of Christ.[22] But I, for one, do not see how they could all be

---

21. Goldingay, *Daniel*, 305.
22. See, e.g., Charles C. Ryrie, *Dispensationalism*, 2d ed. (Chicago: Moody, 2007), 159–60.

fulfilled literally, and the New Testament affirms that some of them have already seen at least partial fulfillment. The apostle Peter claimed that the events on the day of Pentecost in Acts 2 fulfilled the prophecy of Joel 2—but what we see happening in Acts 2 does not correspond closely with what a reader would expect from Joel 2. Or, there's the new covenant prophecy of Jeremiah 31, which the writer of Hebrews so emphasizes (Heb 8). Whereas Hebrews portrays the prophecy as fulfilled in the church, Jeremiah said the new covenant would be made "with the house of Israel and the house of Judah" (Jer 31:31). Is this a literal fulfillment or some type of symbolic fulfillment?

I understand that the various examples I have given of unfulfilled prophecies (blessed future, new covenant, messiah, kingdom) are different from each other in various ways and different from this prophecy about Antiochus Epiphanes in Daniel 11 (assuming it is about him). Yet they seem to indicate that the Christian tradition concerning fulfilled prophecies—going back to the New Testament—does not press the details but instead aligns the overall point of a prophecy with its fulfillment. One more example: I grew up hearing in church that heaven does not really feature a street of gold, despite what we read in Revelation 21:21, where that image is used to indicate beauty and perfection. God did not intend for us to press the details.

The difficulty in applying this normal way of interpreting prophecy to Daniel 11 is that the chapter has been seemingly very precise and accurate about some of the political maneuvering among the Hellenistic dynasties, including the events surrounding Antiochus Epiphanes himself, until verse 40. Whereas Israelite prophecy usually gives impressions (not details) about the future, and even the book of Daniel does this in most other chapters, this particular chapter is almost unique in the Bible (but compare Daniel 8) in providing precise details. So, yes, there are difficulties in saying that the end of Daniel 11 speaks in the language of typical Israelite prophecy; such a characterization of the end of the chapter breaks with the majority of the chapter, which does not fit the normal description of typical Israelite prophecy. But any account of the end of this chapter is going to have its difficulties, especially when we remember that far from being received as a false prophecy it was enshrined as holy Scripture.

Given all these caveats, how might we interpret Daniel 11:40–45 as speaking truthfully about Antiochus Epiphanes? He did cause a lot of mischief up until his last day. His wars continued, as did his persecution of the Jews. And given the historical accounts of his death, connecting his demise with temple robbery, it is easy to evaluate him as an arrogant tyrant who was cut down because of his pride and sacrilege. The prophecy revealed God's truth regarding Antiochus and the divine wrath he would endure, and those who suffered under his regime no doubt rejoiced to see the fulfillment of these words.

Conclusion

What lessons can we derive from Daniel 11? Human governments fight among themselves, they make alliances, they sometimes bring good to people and often bring harm to people, even the best of their citizens, they build up structures and societies that can never be lasting, and yet they exalt themselves, and so it will be until the end of time, until the moment when God puts an end to it.

Discussion Questions

- The man in linen came to tell Daniel about "what is to happen to your people at the end of days" (Daniel 10:14), which turns out to be about some people called "the king of the north" and "the king of the south" (Daniel 11). Who do you think these people are?

- Eventually, the prophecy turns to Antiochus IV Epiphanes, whom we have previously discussed. (He is the little horn in Daniel 8.) Can you tell where the chapter starts talking about Antiochus? What does he do in this chapter?
- Most of Daniel 11 is focused on the kings of the north and south, but the Jewish people are mentioned every once in a while. What happens to the Jewish people in this chapter?
- As in the prophecy of the Seventy Weeks (9:24–27), so also here the phrase "abomination of desolation" is used. Can you tell what this phrase refers to in this prophecy?
- The last ten verses of the chapter (verses 36–45) do not conform well to the career of Antiochus Epiphanes. Many Christians have concluded that the prophecy has now turned its attention to someone else, perhaps the Antichrist at the end of time. What do you think about that way of reading the chapter?

Chapter 12
A New Hope

After life's fitful fever, he sleeps well.
—Macbeth, in *Macbeth* 3.2.24

I 've got good news: we're all going to die! Or, is that even true? The apostle Paul uses the metaphor of sleep for death when he asserts, "We shall not all sleep" (1 Cor 15:51). He means that some people will still be alive on earth when Jesus returns, so those people will not experience death, but the rest of us will. So, let me revise my statement: the good news is that very likely we're all going to die, but if we happen to be alive at the time of the Second Advent, that will be very good, too.

Is death good news? Does the Bible present death as a good thing, as something for which people should long? Usually not. Now, Job did wish that he had been stillborn, for "I would be asleep; then I would be at rest" (Job 3:13), rather than living through the torment his life had become. But even Job recognizes that death is not something to be celebrated. And in the New Testament, death is called an enemy of Christ. But here's the thing: even if "the last enemy to be destroyed is death" (1 Cor 15:26), so that people these days do still experience the horrors of death, we are also assured that death is already now a defeated enemy. After all, Christ shared our flesh and blood "so that through death he might destroy the one who has the power of death, that is, the devil, and free those who all their lives were held in slavery by the fear of death" (Heb 2:14–15).

When Socrates was giving his speech of defense before being condemned to drink the hemlock, he mentioned how little he cared whether he lived or died. "For no one knows whether death be not even the greatest of all blessings to man, but they fear it as if they knew that it is the greatest of evils."[1] You might recall that the apostle Paul had a similar attitude: "To die is gain" (Phil 1:21). A couple of centuries later, Cyprian of Carthage quoted this very passage of Paul and commented that the apostle was

> counting it the greatest gain to be no longer subject to any sins and faults of the flesh, but, released from tormenting afflictions and freed from the poisoned jaws of the devil, to set out, at Christ's summons, for the joy of eternal salvation (*On Mortality* 7).[2]

That sounds to me like good news.

But it is not good news that most ancient Israelites would have known. The idea of the afterlife shared by ancient Israelites —as far as we can glean their thinking from the biblical account and from comparison with the beliefs of other ancient Near Eastern cultures—seems to have been different from the ideas enshrined in the New Testament. That should not be too surprising to the Christian, since it was Jesus "who abolished

---

1. Socrates, in Plato, *Apology* 29a, in the translation of Harold North Fowler, *Plato*, vol. 1, Loeb Classical Library (Cambridge, MA: Harvard University Press, 1914), 107.
2. Translation in Saint Cyprian, *Treatises*, trans. Roy J. Deferrari, Fathers of the Church 36 (New York: Fathers of the Church, 1958), 204. This treatise by Cyprian is briefly summarized by Augustine (*On the Predestination of the Saints* 1.14.26), who also notes the popularity of the treatise.

death and brought life and immortality to light through the gospel" (2 Tim 1:10). The common depiction in the Old Testament of what happens to people when they die involves a place called Sheol and a rather murky and tedious existence. Didn't ancient Israelites believe in the resurrection of the righteous to an eternal reward? Well, modern scholars debate the point, but everyone agrees that the only passage in the Hebrew Bible that clearly displays a hope in the resurrection of the righteous is Daniel 12. In terms of the Old Testament depiction of the afterlife, this chapter of Daniel presents a new hope.

The End of the Vision

The last, brief chapter in the book of Daniel wraps up the vision brought to Daniel by the man in linen, whom we first met in ch. 10 and who might be Gabriel. After his long and detailed report in ch. 11 about the changing fortunes of the kings of the north and the kings of the south, the man in linen announces, finally, that just when all hope seems lost, "Michael, the great prince, the protector of your people, shall arise" (12:1). It is at this point that we read about a resurrection of the righteous, a passage that we will study in a moment. Then the man in linen tells Daniel to keep the vision secret (12:4, cf. 12:9, 8:26). Thus closes the speech of the man in linen.

The rest of the book (12:5–13) is a strange little pericope involving two more angels who interact with Daniel and with the man in linen, revealing that the timing when these things will be accomplished is "a time, two times, and half a time" (12:7, cf. 7:25). Meanwhile, there will be the abomination of desolation (12:11), a phrase we have already encountered twice (9:27, 11:31) and that is always associated with the temple (as also at 1 Macc 1:54, Matt 24:15).[3]

---

3. See Wikipedia: "Abomination of Desolation." According to Alan F. Segal, *Life After Death: A History of the Afterlife in Western Religion* (New York: Random

The Afterlife in the Old Testament

As scholar Jon Levenson has written, "The first transparent and indisputable prediction of the resurrection of the dead in the Hebrew Bible appears in Dan 12:1–3."[4] Indeed, this passage is the first and only such text in the Hebrew Bible. That is not to say that ancient Israelites did not believe in the resurrection; maybe they did, and maybe they didn't. But the idea of a general resurrection of dead people at the end of the age comes through clearly only in a single text. If not resurrection, what ideas about the afterlife predominate in the Hebrew Bible?

Modern Christians are familiar with a place (and a pagan god) called Hades, the place of the dead. The Greek word *hades* appears in the New Testament ten times,[5] including (perhaps most famously) in the Parable of the Rich Man and Lazarus as the residence of the spirit of the rich man after death (Luke 16:23). The word *hades* also appears dozens of times in the Greek Old Testament, usually as a translation for the Hebrew word *sheol*. It is this place, Sheol, which is represented in the Hebrew Bible as the location of the spirits of the dead, basically the equivalent of the Greek Hades.

The word *sheol* appears sixty-five times in the Hebrew Bible, more often in the Psalms than anywhere else. Recent English translations of the Bible often simply use the Hebrew word Sheol in these passages, but some translations, such as the KJV, translate the term as "grave" (e.g., Gen 37:35) or "pit" (e.g., Num 16:30) or some such. But Sheol is not a grave or a pit, it's the supernatural abode of the dead. The residents of Sheol are the

---

House, 2004), 288, the phrase is "a parody of the epithet of Haddad, is a reference to the stationing of Syrian troops in the Temple and the subsequent desecration of Temple purity (Dan 11:31; 12:11). The Syrian troops probably worshipped Haddad in the Jerusalem Temple." On Haddad, see Wikipedia: "Hadad."

4. Jon D. Levenson, *Resurrection and the Restoration of Israel: The Ultimate Victory of the God of Life* (New Haven, CT: Yale University Press, 2006), 181.

5. Matthew 11:23, 16:18; Luke 10:15, 16:23; Acts 2:27, 31; Rev 1:18, 6:8, 20:13–14.

rephaim, often translated "shades."[6] The typical view is that there is no return from Sheol, no emancipation from the place of the dead. Job provides an example.[7]

> As the cloud fades and vanishes,
>> so those who go down to Sheol do not come up;
>> they return no more to their houses,
>> nor do their places know them any more (Job 7:9–10).

Part of the reason that Job's complaint about his situation is so fierce is that he harbors no hope for any vindication beyond death. I know you're thinking of Job 19:25–27, but check out those verses in different translations and you'll find that it's not the kind of passage on which one can rest one's case.[8] Whether there is anything that happens to the human spirit after going to Sheol is a point the Hebrew Bible never raises (except in Daniel 12).

This view of the afterlife in ancient Israel is similar to what we find in the world around Israel. In the *Epic of Gilgamesh*, tablet 7, the friend of Gilgamesh, Enkidu, reports a dream that revealed his fate, which includes a description of the realm of the dead.

> [He trussed] my arms like the wings of a bird,
>> to lead me captive to the house of darkness, seat of Irkalla:
>> to the house which none who enters ever leaves,
>> on the path that allows no journey back,

---

6. The term *rephaim* with the meaning "resident of Sheol" appears nine times in the Hebrew Bible: Isa 14:9, 26:14, 19; Ps 88:10; Job 26:5; Prov 2:18, 9:18, 21:16. See P. S. Johnston, *Shades of Sheol: Death and Afterlife in the Old Testament* (Leicester: Apollos, 2002). There is also another Hebrew word, *rephaim*, that is associated with giants.

7. See also 2 Samuel 12:23; Job 14:1–14, 16:22; Jeremiah 51:39, 57.

8. See N. T. Wright, *The Resurrection of the Son of God* (Minneapolis: Fortress, 2003), 97. For another reading of Job, see Levenson, *Resurrection and the Restoration of Israel*, ch. 4.

to the house whose residents are deprived of light,
>   where dust is their sustenance and clay their food,
>   where they are clad like birds in coats of feathers,
>   and see no light, but dwell in darkness.[9]

Isaiah 14 contains this taunt against the king of Babylon, which uses imagery reminiscent of the scene reported by Enkidu from his dream. Once the king of Babylon experiences the wrath of God, the king will descend to Sheol.

Sheol beneath is stirred up
>   to meet you when you come;
>   it rouses the shades (*rephaim*) to greet you,
>   all who were leaders of the earth;
>   it raises from their thrones
>   all who were kings of the nations.
>   All of them will speak
>   and say to you:
>   "You too have become as weak as we!
>   You have become like us!"
>   Your pomp is brought down to Sheol,
>   and the sound of your harps;
>   maggots are the bed beneath you,
>   and worms are your covering (Isa 14:9–11).

Does everyone go to Sheol, the righteous and the wicked alike? Yes, according to the typical modern scholarly view. Not everyone subscribes to this hypothesis; for instance, Jon Levenson has written a book arguing that Sheol is only for the

---

9. Andrew George, trans., *The Epic of Gilgamesh*, 2d ed. (New York: Penguin, 2020), 59. The vision of the underworld continues further, with Enkidu reporting whom he saw there. See also tablet 12, pp. 148–49 in the translation of George; and see the tale of Ishtar's descent to the underworld in ANET, p. 107. A very similar view of the underworld (i.e., Hades) is found in the Greek world; see, e.g., Homer's *Odyssey* 11.155.

wicked or those rejected by God, whereas the blessed righteous have another destination. What is that destination? "On this, the Hebrew Bible is strikingly silent and forces us into conjecture," Levenson says.[10] While it is always precarious to disagree with Levenson on the interpretation of the Hebrew Bible, I myself lean more toward the traditional view that Sheol is the abode of all the dead, beyond which there is no hope for reward —at least, no hope that God chooses to reveal. But the Hebrew Bible contains scattered exceptions—or possible exceptions, things that make you go "hmm"—such as Enoch (Gen 5:24), or Elijah (2 Kings 2), or Moses (Deut 34), all of whom experienced an end to this life in close association with God. Who knows where they ended up. (That's a statement, not a question.)

If there wasn't a hope for a reward beyond death, what was the ancient Israelite hope? This is the take of biblical scholar N. T. Wright.

> The hope of biblical writers, which was strong and constant, focused not upon the fate of humans after death, but on the fate of Israel and her promised land. The nation and land of the present world were far more important than what happened to an individual beyond the grave.[11]

Such hope for Israel, the people of God, is the most obvious meaning for a biblical passage that uses resurrection as a metaphor: the Valley of Dry Bones in Ezekiel 37. While the dead bones end up growing flesh and coming to life again by means of God's spirit, the point of the prophecy seems to be that the nation Israel, which had gone into exile (= death), would return to their homeland where they would again serve God. Thus they would experience life from the dead. This is not really an explicit

---

10. Levenson, *Resurrection and the Restoration of Israel*, 75. See also Levenson's similar statement on p. 78.
11. Wright, *Resurrection of the Son of God*, 99.

hope for individual resurrection, but rather indicates that the nation Israel would not only continue but—more than that—prosper, would certainly avoid fading into oblivion like so many other nations who experienced exile. The same is true for another passage in the Hebrew Bible sometimes cited in reference to resurrection, Isaiah 26:19.[12]

But ... Daniel 12.

Resurrection

> Many of those who sleep in the dust of the earth shall awake, some to everlasting life, and some to shame and everlasting contempt. Those who are wise shall shine like the brightness of the sky, and those who lead many to righteousness, like the stars forever and ever. (Dan 12:2–3)

As often in the Bible, "sleep" is used as a metaphor for death, and "dust" is the destination of the dead, i.e., Sheol.[13] Uniquely in the Hebrew Bible, the individual people who sleep in the dust wake up. The dead do not stay dead. There is hope for life beyond the grave.

Maybe not for everybody. Does this passage sound to you like it's describing a general resurrection of everybody? Maybe, but it's hard to tell. The passage says "many" will arise.[14] Some

---

12. See Matthias Henze, *Mind the Gap: How the Jewish Writings between the Old and New Testament Help Us Understand Jesus* (Minneapolis: Fortress, 2017), 153–55. Other passages in the Hebrew Bible that might have something to do with resurrection are Isaiah 53:11; Hosea 6:1–3; 13:14. There are also those passages in which someone is raised back to a temporary life (sometimes called resuscitation rather than resurrection); see 1 Kings 17:17–24; 2 Kings 4:1–37; 13:20–21.

13. For some Old Testament examples for "sleep" = death, see 2 Kings 4:31, 13:21; Job 3:13, 14:12; Ps 13:3; Jer 51:39, 57; Nah 3:18. For "dust" as the destination of the dead, see Gen 3:19; Job 10:9, 34:15; Ps 104:29; Eccl 3:20, 12:7; Isa 26:19.

14. It is a common scholarly view that Daniel 12 does not describe a general resurrection; see John J. Collins, *The Apocalyptic Imagination: An Introduction to Jewish Apocalyptic Literature*, 3d ed. (Grand Rapids: Eerdmans, 2016), 140. Maybe the focus of the passage is on Jews.

will rise up to "everlasting life" (the only appearance of that phrase in the Old Testament), others to punishment.

At any rate, the "wise shall shine like the brightness of the sky."[15] There is reward here, unimagined—and no doubt unimaginable—reward, an envisioned transformation of the human person into something new. The wise will not become stars but will shine like them. A Christian reader might recall the brightness of Jesus on the Mount of Transfiguration (Mark 9:3) and the promise that when believers fully see their Lord as he truly is, "we will be like him" (1 John 3:2). I don't know whether anyone knows what Paul had in mind with his talk in 1 Corinthians 15 of a spiritual body—I'm not even sure whether he knew what he had in mind—but it is obviously something radically different from the physical or soulish bodies that we now are. The fact of a radical difference is clear enough from the analogy Paul uses of the seed and the plant, two things closely connected but that look nothing alike (1 Cor 15:36–38). So it is no good asking "How are the dead raised? With what kind of body do they come?" The right response to such questions is, "Thou fool!"

Daniel 12 gives us hope. This is a Jewish hope, of course, and we know that Jews traditionally affirm the doctrine of the resurrection. Not all Jews; we know about the Sadducees (cf. Mark 12:18), who are sad, you see, because there is no life after death. But the dominant form of Judaism for the last couple millennia has affirmed the resurrection, and the Mishnah even classifies this doctrine as an essential aspect of Jewish faith.[16]

This is a Christian hope, and in the Christian approach to resurrection, the process has already started, because Jesus has been raised, having conquered death, thus guaranteeing our own resurrection.

15. On the implications, see Levenson, *Resurrection and the Restoration of Israel*, 189–90, who mentions Paul's "spiritual body" language.
16. See the Mishnah at sefaria.org; look for tractate *Sanhedrin* 10.1.

For if the dead are not raised, then Christ has not been raised. If Christ has not been raised, your faith is futile and you are still in your sins. Then those also who have died in Christ have perished. If for this life only we have hoped in Christ, we are of all people most to be pitied. But in fact Christ has been raised from the dead, the first fruits of those who have died (1 Cor 15:16–20).

Just like the earliest disciples of Jesus (cf. Luke 24:13–35), we put our trust in Jesus and submit to Him not because He died but because He rose, demonstrating His own authority over life and death and everything else (cf. Matt 28:18).

Daniel 12:2–3 provides hope. But it is clear-eyed about that hope. There are some hard days ahead, as the man in linen has revealed to Daniel. While people are running to and fro (12:4),[17] the hope for a life with God provides an anchor to our soul (Heb 6:19). The enemies of God continue, but they shall be put down. "The last enemy to be destroyed is death" (1 Cor 15:26).

Conclusion

The Christian hope, the hope spelled out in the Bible, is that we be united with God, that we glorify God and enjoy Him forever. Daniel 12 presents some new (previously unattested) aspects of that hope. Whereas the majority of the Old Testament exhibits a rather murky vision of what the future holds beyond this life, Daniel 12 provides assurance that God's plans for our well-being do not end at death. Death is an enemy, but a defeated one, not a barrier to the experience of God's grace but a gateway to an experience of grace beyond anything we can imagine now. We have seen that the Bible often describes death as a kind of sleep,

---

17. This verse (Dan 12:4) also says in some translations (following a Greek text) that evil will increase, whereas other translations (following the Hebrew text) say knowledge will increase.

and that metaphor takes on added meaning due to the resurrection of Jesus, who has conquered death, tamed it, made it his slave. As John Donne wrote, "One short sleep past, we wake eternally / And death shall be no more; Death, thou shalt die."

Discussion Questions

- In chapter 12, the "man in linen" (Daniel 10:5) is still talking to Daniel. What does he say will happen at the time of the end (12:1–4)?
- What will happen after a time, times, and half a time?
- What other time periods are given in the final verses, and what will happen at those times?
- The phrase "abomination of desolation" is mentioned several times in our Bibles (Dan 9:27, 11:31, 12:7; Matt 24:15; Mark 13:14). Can you get a sense of what it is, and where it is?
- What is Daniel supposed to do with this revelation? Why?

Bibliography

Adler, William. "The Apocalyptic Survey of History Adapted by Christians: Daniel's Prophecy of 70 Weeks." Pages 201–38 in *The Jewish Apocalyptic Heritage in Early Christianity*. Edited by James C. VanderKam and William Adler. Minneapolis: Fortress, 1996.

Adler, Yonatan. *The Origins of Judaism: An Archaeological-Historical Reappraisal*. New Haven, CT: Yale University Press, 2022.

Adso of Montier-en-Der. *Letter on the Origin and Time of the Antichrist*. Pages 81–96 in *Apocalyptic Spirituality*. Translated by Bernard McGinn. New York: Paulist, 1979.

Ager, Sheila L. "Familiarity Breeds: Incest and the Ptolemaic Dynasty." *Journal of Hellenic Studies* 125 (2005): 1–34.

Almond, Philip C. *The Antichrist: A New Biography*. Cambridge: Cambridge University Press, 2020.

Alstola, Tero. *Judeans in Babylon: A Study of Deportees in Sixth and Fifth Centuries BCE*. Leiden: Brill, 2020.

Anderson, Gary A. *Sin: A History*. New Haven, CT: Yale University Press, 2009.

Appian. *Roman History*. Vol. 1. Translated by Horace White, Loeb Classical Library 2. Cambridge, MA: Harvard University Press, 1912.

Artemidorus. *The Interpretation of Dreams*. Translated by Martin Hammond. Oxford World's Classics. Oxford: Oxford University Press, 2020.

Augustine. *On Christian Teaching*. Translated by R. P. H. Green. Oxford World's Classics. Oxford: Oxford University Press, 1997.

Barclay, John M. G., trans. *Flavius Josephus: Translation and Commentary*, vol. 10: *Against Apion*. Leiden: Brill, 2007.

Bauckham, Richard. *Son of Man*, vol. 1: *Early Jewish Literature*. Grand Rapids: Eerdmans, 2023.

Beaulieu, Paul-Alain. *The Reign of Nabonidus King of Babylon 556–539 B.C.* New Haven, CT: Yale University Press, 1989.

Beckwith, Roger T. "Daniel 9 and the Date of Messiah's Coming in Essene, Hellenistic, Pharisaic, Zealot and Early Christian Computation." *Revue de Qumran* 10 (1981): 521–42.

Begg, Christopher T., and Paul Spilsbury. *Flavius Josephus: Translation and Commentary*, vol. 5: *Judean Antiquities Books 8–10*. Leiden: Brill, 2005.

Braverman, Jay. *Jerome's Commentary on Daniel: A Study of Comparative Jewish and Christian Interpretations of the Hebrew Bible*. Washington, D.C.: The Catholic Biblical Association of America, 1978.

Brown, Derek R. *The God of This Age*. Tübingen: Mohr Siebeck, 2015.

Chapell, Bryan. *The Gospel According to Daniel: A Christ-Centered Approach*. Grand Rapids: Baker, 2014.

Chrysostom, John. *The Cult of the Saints*. Translated by Wendy Mayer and Bronwen Neil. St. Vladimir's Seminary Press Popular Patristics series 31. Crestwood, NY: St Vladimir's Seminary Press, 2006.

Coffman, James Burton. *Commentary on Daniel.* Abilene, TX: ACU Press, 1989.

Collins, John J. *The Apocalyptic Imagination: An Introduction to Jewish Apocalyptic Literature*. 3d ed. Grand Rapids: Eerdmans, 2016.

———. *Daniel: A Commentary on the Book of Daniel*. Hermeneia. Minneapolis: Fortress, 1993.

———. "The Meaning of 'the End' in the Book of Daniel." Pages 91–98 in *Of Scribes and Scrolls: Studies on the Hebrew Bible, Intertestamental Judaism, and Christian Origins*. Edited by H. W. Attridge, John J. Collins, and Thomas H. Tobin. Lanham, MD: University Press of America, 1990).

Conway, J. S. *The Nazi Persecution of the Churches 1933–1945*. Vancouver: Regent College Publishing, 1968.

Cyprian. *Treatises*. Translated by Roy J. Deferrari. Fathers of the Church 36. New York: Fathers of the Church, 1958.

Dalley, Stephanie. *The City of Babylon: A History, c. 2000 BC – AD 116*. Cambridge: Cambridge University Press, 2021.

———. *The Mystery of the Hanging Garden of Babylon: An Elusive World Wonder Traced*. Oxford: Oxford University Press, 2013.

Dan, Anca, and Étienne Nodet. *Cœlé-Syrie: Palestine, Judée*. Leuven: Peeters, 2017.

Davis, Ellen F. *Opening Israel's Scriptures*. Oxford: Oxford University Press, 2019.

Diodorus Siculus. *The Library of History*. Translated by C. H. Oldfather. Loeb Classical Library 279. Cambridge, MA: Harvard University Press, 1933.

Dionysius of Halicarnassus. *Roman Antiquities, Book I–II*. Translated by Earnest Cary. Loeb Classical Library 319. Cambridge, MA: Harvard University Press, 1937.

Driver, S. R. *The Book of Daniel*. Cambridge: Cambridge University Press, 1900.

Eusebius. *The Proof of the Gospel*. Translated by W. J. Ferrar. 2 vols. 1920. Repr. Grand Rapids: Baker, 1981.

Fishbane, Michael. *Biblical Interpretation in Ancient Israel* (Oxford: Oxford University Press, 1985.

Fitzmyer, Joseph A. *The One Who Is to Come*. Grand Rapids: Eerdmans, 2007.

Fowler, Harold North, trans., *Plato*. vol. 1. Loeb Classical Library 36. Cambridge, MA: Harvard University Press, 1914.

Fuller, Robert. *Naming the Antichrist: The History of an American Obsession*. Oxford: Oxford University Press, 1995.

Gallagher, Edmon L. "Daniel and the Dead Sea Scrolls." Pages 410–14 in *Identity in Crisis: Daniel's Vision for the Future: The 81st Annual Freed-Hardeman University Lectureship*. Edited by Doug Y. Burleson. Henderson, TN: Freed-Hardeman University, 2017.

———. "Daniel and the Diadochi." *Journal of Biblical Literature* 141 (2022): 301–16.

———. *The Gospel of Luke: Explorations in Christian Scripture*. Florence, AL: Heritage Christian University Press, 2022.

———. "The Kingdom of God." Pages 154–60 in *Approaching Christian Scripture Faithfully: Twenty Attempts*. Florence, AL: Heritage Christian University Press, 2023.

Gallagher, Edmon L., and John D. Meade. *The Biblical Canon Lists from Early Christianity: Texts and Analysis*. Oxford: Oxford University Press, 2017.

George, Andrew. trans. *The Epic of Gilgamesh*. 2d ed. New York: Penguin, 2020.

Goldingay, John E. *Daniel*. Word Biblical Commentary. Dallas: Word, 1989.

Grabbe, Lester L. *A History of the Jews and Judaism in the Second Temple Period*. 4 vols. London: T&T Clark, 2004–2021.

———. "The Seventy-Weeks Prophecy (Daniel 9:24–27) in Early Jewish Interpretation." Pages 595–611 in *The Quest for Context and Meaning: Studies in Biblical Intertextuality in Honor of James A. Sanders*. Leiden: Brill, 1997.

Grainger, John D. *The Fall of the Seleukid Empire, 187–75 BC*. Barnsley: Pen & Sword, 2015.

———. *The Syrian Wars*. Leiden: Brill, 2010.

Greig, Pete. *How to Pray: A Simple Guide for Normal People*. Carol Stream, IL: NavPress, 2019.

Gurney, Robert M. *God in Control: An Exposition of the Prophecies of Daniel*. West Sussex: H. E. Walter, 198.

Hamilton, Mark W. *A Theological Introduction to the Old Testament*. Oxford: Oxford University Press, 2018.

Hannah, Darrell D. *Michael and Christ: Michael Traditions and Angel Christology in Early Christianity*. Tübingen: Mohr Siebeck, 2009.

Harper, Prudence O., Joan Aruz, and Françoise Tallon, eds., *The Royal City of Susa: Ancient Near Eastern Treasures in the Louvre*. New York: Metropolitan Museum of Art, 1992.

Heckel, Waldemar., and J. C. Yardley. *Alexander the Great: Historical Sources in Translation*. Malden, MA: Blackwell, 2004.

Helm, Rudolf. *Eusebius Werke 7: Die Chronik des Hieronymus*. Die Griechischen Christlichen Schriftsteller der Ersten Jahrhunderte 47. Leipzig: Hinrichs, 1913.

Henze, Matthias. *Mind the Gap: How the Jewish Writings between the Old and New Testament Help Us Understand Jesus*. Minneapolis: Fortress, 2017.

Hesiod. *Theogony; Works and Days; Testimonia*. Edited and translated by Glenn W. Most. Loeb Classical Library 142. Cambridge, MA: Harvard University Press, 2006.

Hurtado, Larry W., and Paul L. Owen, eds., *'Who Is This Son of Man?' The Latest Scholarship on a Puzzling Expression of the Historical Jesus*. London: Bloomsbury, 2011.

Irwin, Brian P., and Tim Perry. *After Dispensationalism: Reading the Bible for the End of the World*. Bellingham, WA: Lexham, 2023.

Jerome. *Commentary on Daniel*. Translated by Gleason L. Archer. Grand Rapids: Baker, 1958.

Johnston, P. S. *Shades of Sheol: Death and Afterlife in the Old Testament*. Leicester: Apollos, 2002.

Justin. *Epitome of the Philippic History of Pompeius Trogus*. Translated by J. C. Yardley. Atlanta: Scholars Press, 1994.

Keil, C. F. *Biblical Commentary on the Book of Daniel*. Repr. Grand Rapids: Eerdmans, 1968.

Kristian, Bonnie. "Confessing Complicity in Systemic Sin." *Christianity Today*. August 20, 2020.

Kusio, Mateusz. *The Antichrist Tradition in Antiquity: Antimessianism in Second Temple and Early Christian Literature*. Tübingen: Mohr Siebeck, 2020.

Ladd, George Eldon. *The Last Things: An Eschatology for Laymen*. Grand Rapids: Eerdmans, 1978.

Larson, Erik. *In the Garden of Beasts: Love, Terror, and an American Family in Hitler's Berlin*. New York: Crown, 2011.

Lee, Harper. *To Kill a Mockingbird*. New York: HarperCollins, 1960.

Lee, James Seung-Hyun. *Reimagining Exile in Daniel: A Literary-Historical Study*. Tübingen: Mohr Siebeck, 2023.

LeFebvre, Michael. *The Liturgy of Creation: Understanding Calendars in Old Testament Context*. Downers Grove, IL: IVP Academic, 2019.

Levenson, Jon D. *Resurrection and the Restoration of Israel: The Ultimate Victory of the God of Life*. New Haven, CT: Yale University Press, 2006.

Lewis, C. S. *The Silver Chair*. The Chronicles of Narnia. New York: HarperCollins, 1953.

Llewellyn-Jones, Lloyd. *Persians: The Age of Great Kings*. New York: Basic, 2022.

Manning, J. G. *The Last Pharaohs: Egypt under the Ptolemies, 305–30 BC*. Princeton: Princeton University Press, 2012.

Marsden, George M. *Fundamentalism and American Culture*, 2d ed. Oxford: Oxford University Press, 2006.

Marsh, Charles. *Strange Glory: A Life of Dietrich Bonhoeffer*. New York: Knopf, 2014.

Mastnjak, Nathan. *Before the Scrolls: A Material Approach to Israel's Prophetic Library*. Oxford: Oxford University Press, 2023.

Maul. Stefan M. *The Art of Divination in the Ancient Near East: Reading the Signs of Heaven and Earth*. Waco, TX: Baylor University Press, 2018.

McGinn, Bernard. *Antichrist: Two Thousand Years of the Human Fascination with Evil*. San Francisco: HarperSanFrancisco, 1994.

McGuiggan, Jim. *The Book of Daniel*. Lubbock, TX: Montex, 1978.

Millard, Alan R. "Daniel in Babylon: An Accurate Record?" Pages 263–80 in *Do Historical Matters Matter to Faith? A Critical Appraisal of Modern and Postmodern Approaches to Scripture*. Edited by James K. Hoffmeier and Dennis R. Magary. Wheaton, IL: Crossway, 2012.

Moberly, R. W. L. *The Bible in a Disenchanted Age: The Enduring Possibility of Chris-

tian Faith. Grand Rapids: Baker, 2018.

Montgomery, James A. *The Book of Daniel.* International Critical Commentary. Edinburgh: T&T Clark, 1927.

Myers, Edward P., Neale T. Pryor, and David R. Rechtin. *Daniel.* Truth for Today. Searcy, AR: Resource, 2012.

Newsom, Carol A., and Brennan W. Breed. *Daniel.* Old Testament Library. Louisville: WJK, 2014.

Origen. *On First Principles: A Reader's Edition.* Translated by John Behr. Oxford: Oxford University Press, 2019.

Plato. *The Republic.* Translated by Tom Griffith. Edited by G. R. F. Ferrari. Cambridge: Cambridge University Press, 2000.

Polybius. *The Histories.* Translated by W. R. Paton. Vol. 6. Loeb Classical Library 278. Cambridge, MA: Harvard University Press, 1927.

Portier-Young, Anathea E. "Languages of Identity and Obligation: Daniel as Bilingual Book." *Vetus Testamentum* 60 (2010): 98–115.

Price, J. Randall. "Prophetic Postponement in Daniel 9 and Other Texts," Pages 133–65 in *Issues in Dispensationalism.* Edited by Wesley R. Willis and John R. Master. Chicago: Moody, 1994.

Pritchard, James B., ed. *Ancient Near Eastern Texts Related to the Old Testament.* 2d ed. Princeton: Princeton University Press, 1955.

Rosenthal, Franz. "*Ṣĕdāqāh*, Charity." *Hebrew Union College Annual* 23 (1950–51): 411–30.

Ryrie, Charles C. *Dispensationalism.* 2d ed. Chicago: Moody, 2007.

Sanders, E. P. *Jewish Law from Jesus to the Mishnah: Five Studies.* Philadelphia: TPI, 1990.

Schäfer, Peter. *Two Gods in Heaven: Jewish Concepts of God in Antiquity.* Princeton: Princeton University Press, 2020.

Schmidt, T. C. *Hippolytus of Rome's Commentary on Daniel.* Piscataway, NJ: Gorgias, 2022.

Segal. Alan F. *Life after Death: A History of the Afterlife in Western Religion.* New York: Doubleday, 2004.

———. *Two Powers in Heaven: Early Rabbinic Reports about Christianity and Gnosticism.* Leiden: Brill, 1977.

Segal, Michael. "The Chronological Conception of the Persian Period in Daniel 9." *Journal of Ancient Judaism* 2 (2011): 283–303.

Seow, C. L. *Daniel.* Westminster Bible Companion. Louisville: WJK, 2003.

Sherwin-White, Susan., and Amélie Kuhrt. *From Samarkhand to Sardis: A New Approach to the Seleucid Empire.* Berkeley: University of California Press, 1993.

Shuck, Glenn W. "Christian Dispensationalism." Pages 515–28 in *The Oxford Handbook of Millennialism.* Edited by Catherine Wessinger. Oxford: Oxford University Press, 2011.

Stokes, Ryan E. *The Satan: How God's Executioner Became the Enemy.* Grand Rapids: Eerdmans, 2019.

Stone, Barton W. "Reflections of Old Age." *Christian Messenger* (August 1843): 123–26.

Tanner, J. Paul. *Daniel*. Evangelical Exegetical Commentary. Bellingham, WA: Lexham, 2020.

Tcherikover, Victor. *Hellenistic Civilization and the Jews*. Philadelphia: JPS, 1959.

Theodoret of Cyrus. *Commentary on Daniel*. Translated by Robert C. Hill. Writings from the Greco-Roman World 7. Atlanta: SBL, 2006.

Tuplin, Christopher. "Medes in Media, Mesopotamia, and Anatolia: Empire, Hegemony, Domination or Illusion?" *Ancient East & West* 3 (2004): 223–51.

———. "Persians as Medes." Pages 235–56 in *Achaemenid History*, vol. 8: *Continuity and Change*. Edited by Heleen Sancisi Weerdenburg, Amélie Kuhrt, and Margaret Cool Root. Leiden: Netherlands Instituut voor het Nabije Oosten, 1994.

VanderKam, James C. *The Dead Sea Scrolls and the Bible*. Grand Rapids: Eerdmans, 2012.

———. *Jubilees*. 2 vols. Hermeneia. Minneapolis: Fortress, 2018.

Walvoord, John F. *Daniel: The Key to Prophetic Revelation*. Chicago: Moody, 1971.

Waterfield, Robin. *Dividing the Spoils: The War for Alexander the Great's Empire*. Oxford: Oxford University Press, 2011.

Waters, Matt. *Ancient Persia: A Concise History of the Achaemenid Empire, 550–330 BCE*. Cambridge: Cambridge University Press, 2014.

———. *King of the World: The Life of Cyrus the Great*. Oxford: Oxford University Press, 2022.

Wheatley, Pat. "Ptolemy Soter's Annexation of Syria, 320 BC." *Classical Quarterly* 45 (1995).

Widder, Wendy L. *Daniel*. Story of God Bible Commentary. Grand Rapids: Zondervan, 2016.

———. *Daniel*. Zondervan Exegetical Commentary on the Old Testament. Grand Rapids: Zondervan, 2023,

Wirzba, Norman. *Food and Faith: A Theology of Eating*. 2d ed. Cambridge: Cambridge University Press, 2019.

Wright, Christopher J. H. *Hearing the Message of Daniel: Sustaining Faith in Today's World*. Downers Grove, IL: IVP, 2017.

Wright, N. T. *Jesus and the Victory of God*. Minneapolis: Fortress, 1996.

———. *The New Testament and the People of God*. Minneapolis: Fortress, 1992.

———. *The Resurrection of the Son of God*. Minneapolis: Fortress, 2003.

Young, Edward J. *The Prophecy of Daniel: A Commentary*. Grand Rapids: Eerdmans, 1949.

Scripture Index

Scripture Index

Ecclesiastes

3:20	178n
12:7	178n

Isaiah

2	166
11:6	165
14	176
14:9	175n
14:9–11	176
26:14	175n
26:19	175n, 178, 178n
39:7	4n
40:21–24	11
45:1	125
53:6	28
53:11	178n
64:6	118
65	166

Jeremiah

1:11–12	55n
10:11	vii
19:1	55n
19:7	55n
23:9–22	163
9:28	163
24:8	40
25:1–14	134
25:9	4
25:11	62n
25:11–12	112
25:13	112n
27:4–7	40
27:6	4
27:17	2
29	106
29:1	62, 112n

29:1–14	134
29:5	112
29:7	62
29:10	62n, 112
29:11	93, 106
29:11–14	116
29:21–22	29n
30:18	125
31	167
31:31	167
31:38–40	125
43:10	4
51:39	175n, 178n
51:57	175n, 178n
52:28	113
52:28–30	3
52:29	113
52:30	113

Ezekiel

1:2	113
2:1	84
29:17–20	166
37	177

Daniel

1	viii–ix
1–6	viii–ix, 116
1:1	114
1:1–2	52
1:1–2:4a	viii
1:2	4
1:3	4
1:4	5, 7, 13
1:5	7
1:6	4
1:7	63
1:8	5

Scripture Index

Scripture Index

Scripture Index

Scripture Index

Also by Ed Gallagher

Hebrew Scripture in Patristic Biblical Theory (Brill, 2012)

The Biblical Canon Lists from Early Christianity (Oxford, 2017) with John D. Meade

The Book of Exodus: Exploration in Christian Theology (Heritage Christian University Press, 2019)

The Sermon on the Mount: Exploration in Christian Practice (Heritage Christian University Press, 2020)

The Gospel of Luke: Exploration in Christian Scripture (Heritage Christian University Press, 2021)

The Translation of the Seventy: History, Reception, and Contemporary Use of the Septuagint (Abilene Christian University Press, 2021)

The Christian Life: Chapters for Bible Teachers (Cypress Publications, 2022)

Jesus the Christ: Chapters for Bible Teachers (Cypress Publications, 2022)

Approaching Christian Scripture Faithfully: Twenty Attempts (Cypress Publications, 2023)

Berean Study Series edited by Ed Gallagher

(HCU Press)

CYPRESS

To see the full catalog of Heritage Christian University Press and its imprint, Cypress Publications, visit www.hcu.edu/publications